HISTORIC WIGTOWN

HISTORIC WIGTOWN

Archaeology and development

R D Oram
P F Martin
C A McKean
S Anderson

THE SCOTTISH BURGH SURVEY

Council for British Archaeology

Published by the Council for British Archaeology and Historic Scotland
First published in 2014

Copyright © 2014 Historic Scotland
The moral right of the authors has been asserted
British Library Cataloguing in Publication Data
A catalogue for this book is available from the British Library

Edited by Catrina Appleby, CBA, and Mark Watson and Martin Brann, Historic Scotland

Page design and typesetting by Carnegie Publishing Ltd

Printing and binding: Berforts Information Press Ltd

ISBN: 978-1-909990-00-5

Council for British Archaeology
St Mary's House
66 Bootham
York YO30 7BZ
www.archaeologyuk.org

Historic Scotland
Longmore House
Salisbury Place
Edinburgh
EH9 1SH
Tel. 0131 668 8600
Fax. 0131 668 8669
www.historic-scotland.gov.uk

Front cover: Wigtown from the air, looking east (Crown copyright: RCAHMS)
Insets: Aquatint by William Daniell of the old harbour, 1815;
the burgh arms, depicting a three-masted ship
Half-title page: The old and new market crosses (Volkmar Nix)

Dedicated to Charles McKean 1946–2013

Charles McKean and his Burgh Survey team colleagues in Fraserburgh in 2007

Contents

Colour broadsheet

List of illustrations

Maps

Figures

List of tables

Abbreviations

CDS	*Calendar of Documents Relating to Scotland*
DES	*Discovery and Excavation in Scotland*
ER	*The Exchequer Rolls of Scotland*
NAS	National Archives of Scotland
NMAS	National Museum of Antiquities of Scotland (now part of the National Museums)
NMRS	National Monuments Record of Scotland
NRAS	National Register of Archives for Scotland
NSA	*The Statistical Account of Scotland* (Edinburgh, 1845)
OSA	*The Statistical Account of Scotland 1791–1799*
PSAS	*Proceedings of the Society of Antiquaries of Scotland*
RCAHMS	Royal Commission on the Ancient and Historical Monuments of Scotland
RMS	*Registrum Magni Sigilli Regum Scotorum*, 11 vols (Edinburgh, 1882–1914)
Rot Scot	*Rotuli Scotiae in Turri Londiniensi et in Domo Capitulari Westmonasteriensi Asservati*
RPC	*Register of the Privy Council of Scotland*, 38 vols (Edinburgh, 1877–)
RRS	*Regesta Regum Scotorum*
RSS	*Registrum Secreti Sigilli Regum Scotorum*
SHS	Scottish History Society
TA	*Accounts of the Lord High Treasurer of Scotland*
TDGNHAS	*Transactions of the Dumfries & Galloway Natural History and Archaeological Society*
Wigtownshire Chrs	*Wigtownshire Charters*

Acknowledgements

We are grateful to Noel Fojut of Historic Scotland for his comments on drafts of this text.

As ever, the staff of the libraries and archives we visited, or which have supplied illustrations, have been friendly and helpful. These include the National Library of Scotland; the National Library of Scotland (Map Library); the National Archives of Scotland; the Royal Commission on the Ancient and Historical Monuments of Scotland; St Andrews University Library; and John Pickin at Stranraer Museum. We are grateful for permission to reproduce images from the British Library, the National Library of Scotland, the RCAHMS and the Ordnance Survey.

We would also like to thank all those we met and spoke to during our field trip, and the book shops we managed to sneak brief visits to.

Introduction to the Survey

The named authors represent the core of a larger team. Kevin Hicks and Leeanne Whitelaw of CFA Archaeology Ltd produced the maps. Fieldwork was carried out in November 2006 by Richard Oram, Charles McKean, Paula Martin and Tim Neighbour, with Colin Martin as a companion and extra photographer. The project was managed for Historic Scotland by Martin Brann and Mark Watson and editing undertaken for the CBA by Catrina Appleby and Frances Mee.

Before the field trip we carried out desk-based historical and archaeological research, so that we arrived with a set of questions. We explored the town on foot, carrying with us copies of the relevant maps and plans, then drove around the immediate hinterland. Charles McKean and Richard Oram had been to the town before, and had spoken to some of those interested in local history. We benefited from meeting a few people during our field trip, and also took the opportunity to read and purchase local publications. John Pickin of Stranraer Museum was also very helpful.

We work as a team, looking for changes in the burgh morphology. We try to spot details and point them out, and bounce ideas off each other (often puzzling passers-by). We look at the backs of as many buildings as possible, and try to identify earlier building- and street-lines. Our aim is to understand the morphology of the town, and its various phases of development, within its physical landscape. Existing architectural guides highlight individual buildings, but we aim to see these buildings within their geographical and historical contexts. We prefer to highlight and explain what still survives, rather than lament a vanished past. Our illustrations concentrate on what we saw and judged important or typical.

After the field visit, more research was carried out on both history and archaeology in the light of a better understanding of the burgh, and the sections on architectural styles and building materials developed. The final section on the 'spirit of place' and potential for further research and sympathetic development was the last to be written. The text contributed by four people has been edited and merged into one narrative, though individual voices will inevitably be apparent in places. The original report was presented to Historic Scotland in spring 2007, and has developed since then in the light of helpful comments from external readers.

Preface: Use of the Burgh Survey

Continued evolution is the essence of urban life. Change is inevitable in towns and is what gives them their vitality. Yet it is the imprint of history that gives localities their distinctive character. Conservation is a matter of ensuring that the qualities that define a place are maintained while change continues to happen. Managing change requires an understanding of that character.

The Scottish Burgh Survey is a guide to the archaeological resource in towns, published by Historic Scotland and the Council for British Archaeology. It helps to influence decision-makers and to set the research agenda on questions that may be answered by archaeology where development occurs. Publications in the latest series are at http://www.archaeologyuk.org/books-and-publications.

This third series of Burgh Surveys is intended to furnish local authorities, developers and residents with reliable information to help manage the archaeology and historic environment of Scotland's urban centres. It offers comprehensive and consistent base-line information against which research, regeneration and land-use planning objectives may be set. It also guides the general reader in researching the rich history and archaeology of Scotland's historic burghs.

In its role as a tool for local authorities to use in the planning process, the first point of reference in this volume is the colour-coded town plan (map 9 and broadsheet) which depicts areas of prime archaeological interest. However, discoveries may yet be made outwith those areas which will necessitate a reassessment of our state of knowledge of the burgh of Wigtown.

Further preliminary research into the archaeological potential of a site within the historic town can be gleaned from local and national libraries and archives. The PASTMAP website (http://www.PASTMAP.org.uk) can also be consulted. This interactive website, supported jointly by Historic Scotland and The Royal Commission on the Ancient and Historical Monuments of Scotland, allows anyone with internet access to search data on Scotland's historic environment including the statutorily protected sites, Scheduled Monuments and Listed Buildings.

Both this Burgh Survey and the PASTMAP website provide information only. Where development is being considered, advice should be sought in all cases directly from Dumfries & Galloway Council Archaeology Service, Planning and Environment, Dumfries & Galloway Council, Militia House, Dumfries, DG1 1LW.

1 Character statement and executive summary

Wigtown was the county town of a moderately sized county, in what now seems a remote corner of Scotland (**maps 1 & 2**). Indeed, in the *Wigtownshire Official Guide* of 1955 it was described as 'probably one of the quietest county towns in Scotland'. This makes its survival and its individual character all the more interesting. It was not always so quiet or so remote, and sufficient traces of a rather more important past remain to help explain the form the burgh takes today.

Its main feature is its large market place or square, a reminder of how important the cattle trade once was to this area. Wigtown's simple river-mouth harbour was important to its economy, as was its early nineteenth-century replacement. So too was a ford across the Cree, which survived until the early nineteenth century (see **map 4**). The town today may seem distant from the main travel arteries of south-west Scotland, but when harbour and ford were functioning it was part of a network of land and sea routes, including a pilgrim route to Whithorn, which fully justified its role as market centre and county town.

The origins of the settlement at Wigtown are uncertain. There is little evidence for prehistoric or early historic occupation on the site, but its location at the western end of the lowest fording point of the Cree on the main east–west route through Galloway perhaps raises the likelihood that it was an early locus of settlement. Tangible evidence of occupation, however, cannot be dated any earlier than the 900s (the remains of a sculpted cross-slab of tenth-century date point to the existence of a Christian community close to the site of the present parish church). By the early thirteenth century, that early settlement had developed into a trading centre with burgh status and a merchant community which was active within a wider Irish Sea network.

Wigtown's emergence as a burgh probably coincided with the formal laying-out of the pattern of streets and burgages which survives as the basis of the current town plan (**map 3**). The settlement was laid out on a slightly sloping, south-facing terrace on the southern edge of a promontory of high ground which extends along the north side of the valley of the River Bladnoch. While the High Streets of a number of burghs are also on slopes (Brechin and Whithorn for example), and other burghs have height differences between the two sides of the main street (for example Montrose, Newburgh and Cupar), the sheer size of the central space in Wigtown, combined with the slope, means that at its east end, one side of the principal market place is up to a storey higher than the other.

Its north-east to south-west alignment was probably largely dictated by the topography of the site and a pre-existing trackway running across it. The

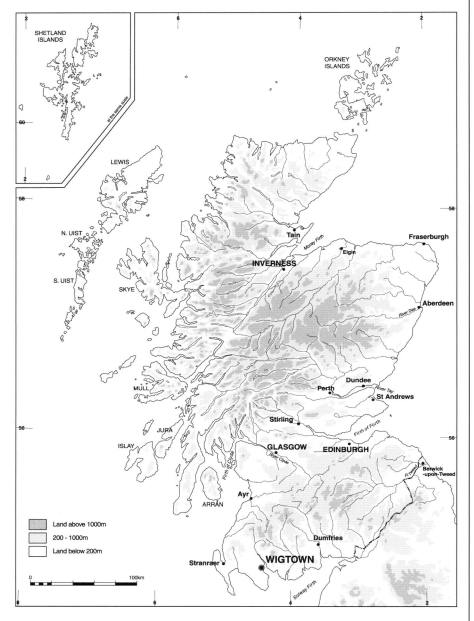

MAP I
Location of Wigtown

road from the former ford and harbour climbs a steep slope and enters the burgh at the East Port just past the suburban parish church. At the crest of the hill, the road debouches into the great central space of the burgh beside the former site of the tolbooth and market cross: the medieval business centre. The 'Square' itself is a great trapezoidal space, wider at the north-east than at the south-west, and with access at both ends once closed by ports. These originally formed an area whose enclosed character has been blown open by the eighteenth-century demolition of the ports, the driving of roads through its northern edge in the nineteenth century, and the creation of gaps in the

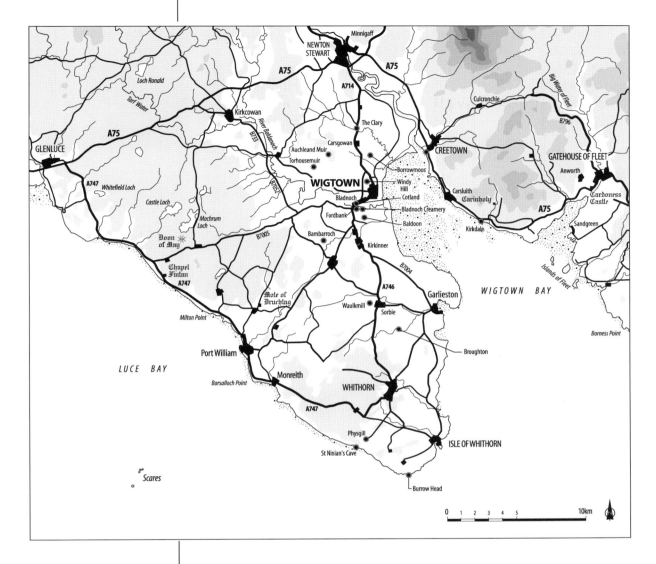

MAP 2
Wigtown and its hinterland

street frontage on the south side in the nineteenth and twentieth centuries. Beyond the Square the roads to the west and south-west narrow rapidly and the built-up area of the burgh ends abruptly in both directions as the land falls away to the low ground by the Bladnoch.

Most visitors today enter the town from the north, and perhaps the most striking aspect of their approach is the manner in which they suddenly emerge into the central open space part-way along one side. Rather than progressing along a ribbon development extending out from one of the burgh's former ports, entry is quite abrupt and runs against the grain of the plan's main axis. This unusual entry is a consequence of the gradual decline and abandonment of the ancient lines of approach – from the ford and old harbour to the north-east; from Whithorn via the Bladnoch bridge to the south-west; and from Stranraer to the west – in favour of the route south from the Cree bridge at Newtown Stewart. This reorientation of travel networks, which began in the early 1700s, led to the road from the north entirely replacing the ancient routeway from the east, while travellers to Stranraer cross the Cree at Newton Stewart and continue west, and those heading for Whithorn now also bypass the town. One consequence of this reorientation was a shift in emphasis within the burgh from the east end to the west. To the modern visitor, this development is most evident in the clustering of commercial premises, banks and hotels round the staggered crossroads where New Road crosses the Square towards Agnew Crescent or High Street, contrasted with the now almost entirely residential and administrative character of the east end of the Square.

MAP 3
Detail of Roy map (1747–55) showing the burgh (Reproduced by permission of the Trustees of the British Library)

Executive summary

➤ Both the geographical location of the town, and its morphology, are unusual.

➤ The town centre consists of a large triangular market place, once gated at both ends; it appears that the gates enclosed not the whole burgh but just its market place.

➤ The burgh's main street is aligned on the former ford from Creetown, once the main east–west route through Galloway and part of a pilgrimage route to Whithorn.

➤ Created a royal burgh in the later thirteenth century, in 1341 it was downgraded to a burgh of regality belonging to the newly created Earl of Wigtown, then passed in 1372 to the Douglas family. The town formally regained its royal burgh status following the forfeiture of the earldom of Douglas in 1455.

➤ In the later medieval and early modern period there was competition between Wigtown and Whithorn, which had a better port at the Isle, to handle exports from their limited hinterland. Eventually Garlieston overtook both.

➤ After the Cree was bridged further north (and the ford went out of use), a new road was laid out running north, intruding on the enclosure of the central market place.

➤ After the river-mouth moved, a new harbour and then the railway station were built to the south, further changing the dynamics of the town, though both have now gone.

➤ As in many burghs, the church stood outside the boundary, but it was not moved, nor did the town expand to enclose it.

➤ The fortunes of Wigtown, like those of many other small Scottish towns, declined as transport networks improved from the early nineteenth century.

Timeline

10th century	Early church in existence
Early 13th century	Wigtown burgesses named in the freedom rolls of Dublin
1265	First surviving mention of the royal castle
c 1267	Foundation of Dominican friary by Dervorgilla Balliol
1296–c 1312	English garrison holds the castle
1341	Burgh included as 'chief place' within the earldom of Wigtown created for Malcolm Fleming, losing its royal burgh status
1372	Thomas Fleming sells lands of the earldom to Archibald Douglas 'the Grim' and surrenders his title to the king. Wigtown passes into Douglas control
1455	Forfeiture of earldom of Douglas and re-establishment of the town as a royal burgh
1457	Confirmation of the privileges of Wigtown as a royal burgh by James II
1501–07	James IV lodges in burgh during pilgrimages to Whithorn
1510	Start of legal disputes with Whithorn over trade
1560	Friary lands feued to Sir Alexander Stewart of Garlies
1587	First surviving mention of a tolbooth
1633	Date of earliest surviving bell
1662	Re-issue and expansion of burgh charter, granting the right to charge tolls on all cattle, sheep and wool crossing the Cree
1705	Establishment of post office
1712	New building for grammar school
1728	First stone bridge over the River Bladnoch
1730	Parish church rebuilt
1747	Old tolbooth demolished and work started on new one
1750	Antiburgher meeting house built
1761	Removal of East and West Ports
1776	Rebuilding of Town House
1784	Branch of Bank of Scotland opened
1794	Establishment of subscription library
1795	Establishment of Friendly Society
1797	Formation of Volunteers
1809	The Square formally laid out
1812	Bowling green laid out in the Square
1816	New market cross, establishment of Gas Company

1822	New harbour opened
1825	Start of steamer services
1830	Founding of Wigtown Bowling Club
1843–44	Free Church built
1845	United Secession Church built, and new parish school
1846–48	New prison built
1851	New parish church built
1858	Covenanters Monument erected
1862–63	County Buildings and new Town Hall constructed
1867	New bridge over Bladnoch
1873	Oddfellows Lodge established
1875	Arrival of railway
1879	Roman Catholic church built
1887	The Square remodelled, with new bowling green
1899	Bladnoch Creamery opened
1903	Masonic Lodge re-established
1930	New, improved water supply and drainage
1950	Railway closed for passenger services
1959	Establishment of golf course
1997	Created Scotland's first 'Book Town'

2   Site and setting

'The royal burgh of Wigton is a small decent town, situated near the mouth of a stream called Bladenoch, on an eminence at a considerable elevation from the sea. In this respect it differs from the small towns on the coast, which are generally situated in valleys'[1] (**map 4; fig 1**). Wigtown sits about 200 feet above sea-level, 'commanding an extensive view of the bay of Wigton, of the stewartry of Kirkcudbright, of the distant hills of Cumberland, and of the Isle of Man'.[2] The apparent peculiarity of its site in relation to water-supply and lines of communication has long attracted comment, it being observed that 'The physical character and even the position of early Wigtown remain something of a mystery'.[3] Andrew Symson recorded in 1684 the local belief that the town was originally called 'Danewort' and 'of old stood more than a mile Eastward but that place is now covered with the sea every tide'.[4] Antiquarian puzzles about the location of the earliest settlement were spurious, however, and it is perhaps worth noting that Peter M'Kerlie, the principal local historian of the nineteenth century, rejected Symson's

MAP 4
Physical setting of Wigtown

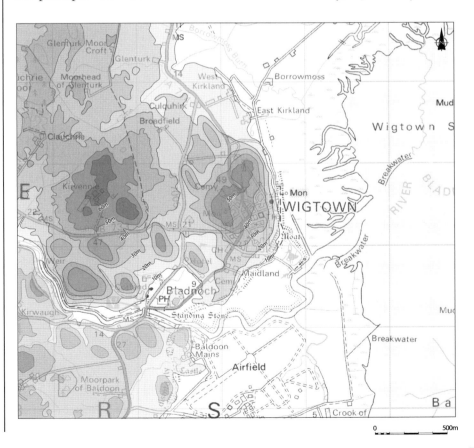

0　　　　　500m

FIGURE I
Air photograph showing
Wigtown in its geographical
setting (28 May 1966)
(© Crown copyright
Ordnance Survey. All rights
reserved)

suggestion, regarding the present situation, up on the hill, as a much more logical site for a burgh to have grown up.[5] Nevertheless, Symson's belief may well reflect a local feeling that the site of the town was unusual.

The fundamental point about Wigtown is that it was located and orientated to serve one of the principal east–west transport routes of south-west Scotland, which entered the town from the north-east from the ferry and low-water ford on the Cree and exited to the west and south-west, which made it part of an important pilgrimage route to Whithorn. Main Street is aligned on the ford, which solves previous questions about the town's layout.[6] Apart from a possible secondary focus for settlement around the castle on the low ground to the south of the town, all the evidence suggests that the burgh of Wigtown was always located on its present site. The ford across the Cree is clearly marked on William Roy's map of *c* 1750 (**map 5**). Daniell, describing the eastern shore of the estuary, observed that 'people at low water may walk two or three miles across the sands to Wigton, though from the intervention of several small rivers, and the wetness of the sands, the passage is very disagreeable'.[7] The ferry appears to have been withdrawn by the time he was writing, perhaps once the Cree had been bridged at Minigaff in 1703.

Such an open site was considered 'naturally healthful',[8] and the burgh was well sheltered from the north. The climate was mild in the winter, but relatively cool in summer. 'The gentle breezes which arise from the sea,

help to preserve the temperature of the air, and render the weather more moderate than could otherwise be expected in so northern a situation. … The greatest defect … arising, no doubt, from the proximity of the sea, is an inconstancy of weather.' There was plenty of fresh water, enough wind to drive away the damp, and snow and frosts did not last long. The land was fertile: 'the soil is here, both on the hills and plains, a dry, light, hazle mould, lying in some places on a bed of till, and in other places on a bed of gravel'.[9] A combination of climate and post-glacial geomorphology, however, produced potential arable land only under about 500 feet. Much of the surrounding land, characterised formerly by rocky outcrops interspersed with glacial kettle-holes and infilled fen, is better suited to pastoral farming.[10] The mild winter weather allowed cattle to be left outside, reducing the cost of both shelter and food.

Situated on the eastern border of Wigtownshire, and on the western shore of Wigtown Bay, the town is 13km (8 miles) from Newton Stewart, 45km (28 miles) from Stranraer, and 93km (58 miles) from Dumfries. Wigtown had a small harbour, but the large tidal range, combined with silting, made the harbours north and east of Garlieston increasingly difficult of access. As the size and draught of ships increased, and steam replaced sail, many ports fell out of use, with Stranraer the main survivor. The railways gradually replaced coastal shipping, and long-distance travel routes changed with the development of turnpike roads, then the advent of steam shipping, then railways, and most recently with the demise of the railways and coastal shipping, and the development of trunk roads.

Building materials and details

Wigtown stands on a peninsula of the Silurian rock which underlies most of the Machars, with marine alluvium both sides of it. The most common local rock is the hard, slate-like multi-coloured grey-orange greywacke, a type of indurated sandstone occurring in beds of various thicknesses, which was

9

the predominant building stone (**figs 2 & 3**), although difficult to carve.[11] Seventeenth-century gravestones were mostly of whinstone. Sandstone later became dominant, particularly for finer work, until the introduction of machine-cut granite *c* 1890.[12] The sandstone seems most likely to have come by sea from Dumfries or Whitehaven, initially greyish, but by the mid-nineteenth century a deep-red sandstone was used, particularly for dressings. A few houses, particularly in Bank Street, are constructed of greywacke with red sandstone dressings as in Whithorn. The later nineteenth century saw a greater use of granite (**figs 2 & 3**) and a not infrequent use of brick, particularly for outhouses. An increasing number of the town's houses have been painted recently, obscuring their materials. Only occasionally are they harled, although there is some evidence that this had been the coating in earlier centuries.

Thatch was used widely for roofing, although slate was beginning to predominate by the mid-nineteenth century. Wigtown, like Whithorn, has a number of buildings roofed in the English rather than the Scottish manner, with flat slates and an absence of skews – as, for example, 4 High Street. Perhaps as a result, crowsteps are rare.

The name of the town

The name used on earlier maps is 'Wigton'. As the volume of postal communication increased during the nineteenth century, a problem arose as to

FIGURE 2
Typical construction of a mix of granite and roughly coursed greywacke, with painted window and door surrounds. The central pend has been infilled (Paula Martin)

FIGURE 3
The Masonic Hall, Agnew Crescent, built of rectangular blocks of greywacke with some cherry-cocking, and granite dressings. The ten-panelled doors are a local characteristic, but the original slate roof has been replaced by concrete tiles (Paula Martin)

how to distinguish between Wigton in Wigtonshire and Wigton in Cumbria, and it was decided that the Scottish town should spell its name 'Wigtown'. It is clear, however, that this alone did not prevent confusion, and during the second half of the century the following note appears in Trades Directories: 'Attention is directed to the necessity of addressing letters "Wigtown, North Britain" or "Wigtown, Wigtonshire" [sic], not Wigton (only), as in the latter case letters will be forwarded to Wigton, in Cumberland, instead of their proper destination'.

Note on the burgh arms

One of the key questions about Wigtown is how important was its role as a port. It is interesting that its arms depict a three-masted merchant sailing ship (**fig 4**). A survey of other burgh arms yielded several rowing boats (for example Pittenweem and Wick), and several simplified medieval ships (for example Kirkcudbright), but only a few larger ships. The ships on the arms of Greenock, and a secondary coat of arms of Leith, are eighteenth-century or later (and the Leith ship flies an English flag). The Kirkwall ship is odd, but could be sixteenth-century. The Wigtown, Burntisland and Stranraer ships all have a three-masted rig, with lower and top sails on the main- and foremasts, a lateen on the mizzen-mast, with a square topsail, and a short mast with a square sail set on the bowsprit. This feature suggests a date for the rig of late sixteenth to early seventeenth century. However, some versions of the Wigtown ship display archaic elements of fifteenth-century character, which could suggest that the seal was designed after the town became a royal burgh again in 1455.[13] It also suggests that the town at that date clearly saw itself as a port.

FIGURE 4
The burgh arms, depicting a three-masted ship

Notes

1 W Daniell, *Daniell's Scotland: a Voyage around the Coast of Scotland and the Adjacent Isles, 1815–22*, 2 vols (Edinburgh, 2006), **i**, 62.

2 *The Statistical Account of Scotland* (Edinburgh, 1845), 'Parish of Wigton', Revd Peter Young, 1839, 1.

3 G Stell, *Dumfries and Galloway* (HMSO, 1986), 69.

4 A Symson, *A Large Description of Galloway by Andrew Symson, Minister of Kirkinner, 1684* (Edinburgh, 1823), 34; also in W Macfarlane, *Geographical Collections relating to Scotland* (Mitchell, A and Clark, J T eds, Edinburgh, 1906–08), **ii**, 72–4.

5 P H M'Kerlie, *History of the Lands and their Owners in Galloway*, 5 vols (Edinburgh, 1870, repr, ed Gardner, 2 vols, Paisley, 1906), 158.

6 A Graham, 'Some old harbours in Wigtownshire', *TDGNHAS*, 3rd ser **54** (1979), 69–74.

7 Daniell, *Daniell's Scotland*, **i**, 56.

8 *The Statistical Account of Scotland 1791–1799, v, Stewartry of Kirkcudbright and Wigtownshire*, eds D J Withrington and I R Grant (Wakefield, 1983), 'Parish of Wigton', Revd Andrew Duncan (1793), 566.

9 *OSA*, 557–8.

10 I Morrison, 'Galloway: Locality and Landscape Evolution', in R D Oram and G P Stell eds, *Galloway: Land and Lordship* (Edinburgh, 1991), 13–14.

11 *Third Statistical Account of Scotland, The County of Wigtown*, ed M C Arnott (Glasgow, 1965), parish of Wigtown, Revd Gavin Lawson, 1949 and 1963, 342, 344.

12 J E Birchman, typescript record of Wigtown Old Churchyard, Tombstone Inscriptions (1981), courtesy of John Pickin, Stranraer Museum.

13 Colin Martin, pers comm. A Lindsay, *A Rutter of the Scottish Seas c 1540* (National Maritime Museum Mongraphs **44**, 1980), 17, the editors highlight it as an image of a transitional 16th-century type of 3-masted vessel; A Murray, 'The Customs Accounts of Kirkcudbright, Wigtown, and Dumfries, 1434–1560', *DGNHAS* **xl** (1963), facing 136, a sketch of a 3-masted ship appears in the burgh court book in 1522.

3   Archaeology and history

Prehistory

Although the Bladnoch valley to the west of the burgh is rich in Neolithic and Bronze Age monuments, most famously the stone circle and cairns at Torhouse, very little prehistoric evidence has so far been found in the immediate environs of Wigtown itself. The only recorded monument is a standing stone at nearby Bladnoch. This granite boulder is incorporated into the wall which lines the south side of the village street.[1]

Some lithic artefacts were collected at unlocated findspots in the nineteenth century. Three of these were given to the National Museum of Antiquities of Scotland in 1880 and 1889. The 1880 find is a yellowish claystone hammer from 'the neighbourhood of Wigtown', measuring approximately 145 x 95 x 70mm with a perforation *c* 30mm in diameter at its narrowest.[2] Those accessioned in 1889 were axe-hammers, one measuring *c* 205 x 110mm and the other *c* 185 x 85mm.[3] Petrological analysis has shown that one (NMS AH 81) was of greywacke from the Southern uplands and the other (NMS AH 83) was of Essexite from central Ayrshire.[4] A further perforated greywacke axe (*c* 200 x 130 x 70mm) from Wigtown was bought by Sir Herbert Maxwell of Monreith in 1880.[5] That all four recorded objects were axes perhaps provides more of an insight into the preferences of Victorian collectors than into the prehistory of the area. The petrological analysis does at least provide some clues about the trade links in the region during the Neolithic, and the finds suggest that there is a high potential for more prehistoric archaeology in the area.

Roman

The only known find of Roman date from the area is a copper-alloy coin of Hadrian, which was found in the garden of 3 South Main Street in 1967.[6] Stray finds of Roman coins may be attributable to casual loss and do not necessarily indicate the presence of a site of the period, but this would need to be tested by excavation. Roman material is well attested on excavated native sites of the period in western Galloway, such as Rispain near Whithorn,[7] perhaps indicating a high level of interaction between the Roman province and the tribes beyond the frontier, but whether it was obtained through trade, raid or subsidy remains a matter of debate.

Early historic and medieval archaeology

Early origins for the settlement at Wigtown were hinted at by the discovery of part of a tenth-century cross-shaft in the parish churchyard (**fig 5**).[8] Symson, writing in 1684, claimed that the former settlement (he gives the old name as *Epiack* or *Epiacte*) lay more than a mile eastward in an area which was then covered by the sea 'at every tide'.[9] This would be within the saltings. If there was an area of pre-burghal settlement, it seems more likely that its focus would have been the church. This was largely rebuilt in 1730 on foundations probably laid in the twelfth or thirteenth century (see **fig 10**).[10] The corner buttresses, chamfered plinth, string-course and blocked windows of the medieval church are still visible at the east end (**fig 6**).[11] The tenth-century cross may point to an earlier church here (or perhaps elsewhere in the parish), as may the record of a possible Romanesque-style font which was noted by Muir in 1849, but which was no longer present in 1864.[12]

The main phase of activity at Wigtown Castle has been dated to between *c* 1260 and *c* 1315,[13] although traditionally it is thought to have been constructed as a controlling measure following a revolt by the men of Galloway in 1235 (see below for more detail). It was originally situated by the river, which has since changed its course, and its ditch on the west and north sides was filled by the tide. No ditch was required on the east and south owing to the proximity of the sea. The site was sub-circular with a wall of stone and lime, and the ditch was *c* 9m wide and 3m deep. The outer wall and ditch were uncovered during excavations by Captain R M'Kerlie in 1830,[14] and it was also discovered that the main gate and drawbridge were located on the south-western side. The interior has since been quarried. The site is the only Scheduled Monument in the burgh (**fig 7**).[15]

The two town gates, the East and West Ports, were demolished in 1761.[16] The site of the West Port was recorded on the 1896 OS map (**map 6b**), and traces were still extant in the 1950s.[17] It stood between buildings which projected on either side, one of which survived to be noted in 1877.[18] The East Port is less well recorded but is believed to have stood at the east end of Bank Street, probably just west of the mouth of Church Lane which divides the north side of the street from the churchyard.

There has been a long debate, still unresolved, over the location of the burgh's thirteenth-century Dominican friary. Writing in the late seventeenth century, the local minister, Andrew Symson, had described its very fragmentary remains as 'lying on the south-east of this town'.[19] However, by the nineteenth century M'Kerlie said the friary was located 'close to the east end of the town, on a small eminence near

FIGURE 5
Part of a tenth-century cross-shaft found in the parish churchyard (© RCAHMS)

FIGURE 6
The east end of the medieval
church (Martin Brann)

the mouth of the river Bladenoch'. All traces were by then gone, and the site 'converted into a field or orchard, and known as Croft-an-Righ'. This area, which lies part-way down the hill between the north-east end of the burgh and the former harbour on the route to the Cree ford, was said to contain a portion of standing wall in 1818, when there were also tan-pits on the ground.[20] The tan-pits were noted in 1970 on the site of three ruined buildings marked on the first edition OS map (1850) at the foot of the slope south of Croft-an-Righ (**map 6a**).[21] A further ruined building is recorded to the north.[22] M'Kerlie claimed that the entrance was from the north, through a large arched gateway over which hung a bell; this was known as the Bell Yett, but nothing remained of it in his time. He also recorded the presence of the Friars' Well, which had a stone wall and associated lead pipes in the eighteenth century.[23] He stated that human remains had been found to the north and east of this site. This could perhaps be accounted for if the church of St Machutus was an early foundation which had originally had a much more extensive graveyard.

Alternative sites were proposed for the friary in the later twentieth century. The OS record of 1970 suggested that it may have been situated further to the south-west, within the grounds of Bank House,[24] but the evidence for this is unclear. The site is marked on the second edition OS map (though not on the town plan of 1848) in a field to the east of the town, on the south side of the road near the church. This field has produced bone and ceramics following ploughing.[25] A substantial wall delineating the south end of this large field, which is suggested to have formed the boundary of the friary grounds, was

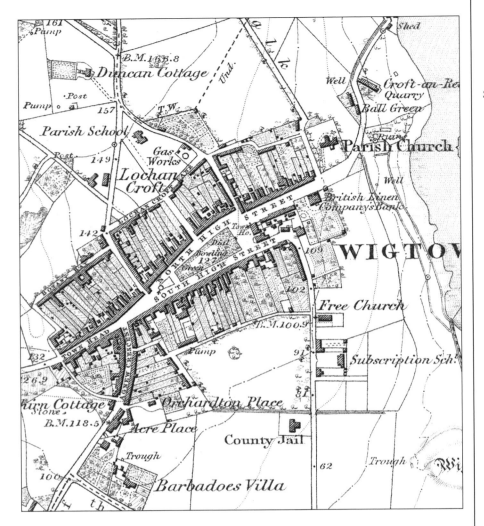

FIGURE 7
The castle site, the slight mound on which the cattle are standing (Richard Oram)

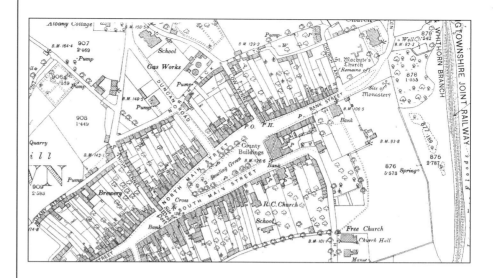

recorded in 2001 when its south face was revealed by garden works to the rear of Kirkston on Harbour Road.[26] In December 2002, the field itself was investigated by geophysical survey and a series of anomalies was found; these were interpreted as small-scale footings for buildings, ditches and walls/ paths, some of which may have been boundaries for the friary cemetery.[27]

These interpretations, however, are formulated partly on the assumption that the friary stood at this location.

The precise site marked on the OS map, however, is on a considerable slope, making it unlikely to have been the core of the friary. Further uncertainty arises from a burgh council minute of 1717, which refers to a 'Freir vennald' (vennel).[28] This description appears to refer to the south back vennel, which might indicate a site somewhere in the vicinity of the South Field or the properties at the northern end of Harbour Road, a location which would tally better with Symson's account. Harbour Road was opened between Main Street and the new harbour c 1820. Built into the wall on its western side, by the South Field, is a significant quantity of late medieval moulded stonework of uncertain provenance, whereas none was found in the walls east of Bank Street where the OS located the Friary. However recent trial trenching in South Field itself produced no evidence of any structures or settlement. The precise location of the friary, therefore, remains a puzzle.

The gardens of the current house called Croft-an-Righ contain a stone pillar, found in the garden but of uncertain origin, on one face of which are incised two crosses in the style of the thirteenth century (**fig 8**).[29] Given its proximity to St Machutus church and the possible location of the friary, it seems likely that the object originally belonged to one of these institutions.

Within the town, none of the existing street frontages suggests the survival of any houses or commercial buildings older than the later seventeenth or early eighteenth century. Internal building work at 11 North Main Street in 2001, however, revealed a large fireplace and wall cupboard in the north gable. Several blocked windows and an entrance in the east wall were also recorded, and showed that the house had originally been at least three storeys high. The core of the structure was revealed to be an L-shaped late medieval townhouse.[30]

Stonework of late medieval or early post-medieval date has been recorded in two of the town's houses. A pink freestone slab inscribed 'HK ES 1661' is built into the rear of 10 North Bank Street, and the gable of its kitchen wing contains a carved human head (**fig 9**).[31] The latter could perhaps be reclaimed from one of the ecclesiastical establishments or the castle. At 17 Agnew Crescent, a relief-carved panel showing an arcade with figurative work was found built into an outhouse to the rear of the property.[32] Again it is likely to be recycled from a demolished building.

Archaeological recording during development work has been possible at only a few sites around the town to date. At 26 South Main Street, the removal of an extension in 1997 allowed for observation of the underlying layers and revealed that the ground had probably been levelled in post-medieval times, removing all but a small portion of the medieval deposits.[33] Observation of trenches to the south-west side of High Vennel in 1992 also failed to reveal any medieval layers;[34] this area was a garden at the time of the first edition OS map. A watching brief during 2002 in the public gardens between North and South Main Street revealed nineteenth- or twentieth-century tip deposits.[35] Three other watching briefs located towards the rear of three of the town's burgage plots have revealed only recent garden soils overlying natural bedrock. These were at 4 Lochancroft Lane,[36] land to the rear of the Baptist Church on Southfield Lane,[37] and further to the east on Southfield Lane.[38]

FIGURE 9
Carved human head on a skewput at the back of No 10 North Bank Street (Richard Oram)

Medieval history

Establishment of the burgh

Traditionally, the origins of Wigtown as a burgh have been dated to the period following the absorption of Galloway into the kingdom of Scotland after the death of Alan, Lord of Galloway, in 1234. It has been said that the establishment of the royal castle and burgh at Wigtown was a consequence of the suppression of a revolt by the men of Galloway in 1235, which saw King Alexander II plant castles at Wigtown and Kirkcudbright as part of a new mechanism for tighter royal control. Burghs, however, appear to have existed at both locations prior to 1234, and were probably the creation of Alan of Galloway or his father, Roland (d.1200). Already by the early thirteenth century there appears to have been a developed burgess community at Wigtown with trading contacts around the Irish Sea, two men 'of Wiketune' being named as burgesses in the Dublin Guild Merchant Roll alongside five Kirkcudbright men and three others from Galloway.[39] Although Wigtown is not named in any surviving documents as representing a component of the personal estates of Alan of Galloway and his predecessors, the possession of property there by his daughter, Dervorgilla, suggests that they may have been direct lords of the community here before its formal institution as a burgh.[40]

At the time of its emergence as a burgh in the later twelfth or early thirteenth century, Wigtown was probably awarded control of an extensive range of material rights in addition to the normal economic and fiscal privileges. It is likely, for example, that it was given exclusive rights to exploit natural resources within its hinterland, such as timber for building and, possibly, for fuel, but certainly peat from the mosses to the north for domestic and industrial hearths. References to the burgh's resources are rare in the records, but sixteenth- and seventeenth-century accounts make it clear that access to scarce timber supplies and security of fuel supplies were jealously guarded privileges.

The creation of the sheriffdom of Wigtown was a result of the integration of Galloway into the kingdom of the Scots after Alan of Galloway's death in 1234, but how soon remains a matter of debate. It has been suggested that it may have followed close on the heels of the suppression of a regional revolt in 1235 which aimed at preventing the partition of the lordship between Alan's three heiresses and their husbands.[41] Equally, it could have been a consequence of the crown's involvement in suppressing a second rebellion in 1247 against Roger de Quincy, Earl of Winchester, the husband of the senior heiress, whose harsh government was said to have provoked the rising.[42]

At the exchequer audit for 1265, Alexander Comyn, Earl of Buchan and sheriff of Wigtown, accounted for 40 merks which he had been allocated to cover repair work on 'houses' within the castle of Wigtown.[43] From this 100s had been retained due to faults, perhaps caused by the speed with which the work was undertaken, as 5 merks were remitted to the master mason 'on account of the completion of the works made against the coming of the Norwegians'. It has been said that this is unlikely to refer to the hasty preparations made to withstand the expected invasion of Scotland by the Norwegians under King Haakon IV in 1263,[44] but given the continued warfare in the Western Isles through 1264 and the fact that the Scoto-Norwegian negotiations which led to the Treaty of Perth began in earnest only in 1265, that possibility cannot be ruled out.

Alternatively the work may have been undertaken in advance of the arrival of a Norwegian embassy for those treaty negotiations and, although it may seem odd that such a delegation should arrive in Scotland at a remote south-western port, it is possible that it had first to undertake business touching on the future fate of the kingdom of Man.[45] Negotiations between the Scots and King Magnus Ólafsson of Man were certainly under way by 1264, when Magnus came to Dumfries to give homage to Alexander III. In his 1266 account Alexander Comyn recorded the expenses of the Archdeacon of Man and a party of Dominicans, possibly but not certainly from the community at Wigtown, going twice to Man on the king's business in 1265, and a second item for expenses of the canons of Whithorn, the archdeacon and sixteen men also going to Man.[46]

The castle

It is likely that the royal castle at Wigtown, like that at Kirkcudbright, was secondary to the development of the burgh rather than forming the focus from which the settlement stemmed. Its location on the low ground to the south-east of the burgh suggests that its purpose was to control the harbour and river-mouth. Apart from references to repairs in the 1260s, little is known of its history until a brief period of activity between 1290 and 1305, after which it disappears from the documentary record.

The castle was probably one of the targets against which the Bruce family moved in the autumn of 1286 as it manoeuvred for power following the death of Alexander III. Held as it was by John Comyn, Earl of Buchan, who had succeeded his father, Alexander, as sheriff of Wigtown, the Bruces were also striking against a key asset of one of the greatest allies of their Balliol rivals. The raid into Wigtownshire led by Robert Bruce, Earl of Carrick, appears to have been highly destructive, with possibly even the cathedral-priory at Whithorn suffering in the attack.[47] In his exchequer account for 1288–90, Earl John did not respond for 'that land which lies uncultivated on account of the war moved by the Earl of Carrick', which might suggest that there had been widespread dislocation of normal life and a loss of population which had still not been made good some years later.[48] There is little further evidence for any major role played by the castle, though it remained a symbol of crown authority in the sheriffdom.

During Edward I's oversight of the Scottish administration in 1290–92, regular records survive of payments made to English knights who were appointed as keepers of the royal castles. Dumfries, Kirkcudbright and Wigtown castles were all placed under the keepership of one man, who would have been responsible for installing suitable constables to act for him locally. The keeper in 1290–91 was Sir William de Boyville, who received the substantial wages of 1 merk daily, plus expenses for the maintenance of his retinue.[49] Boyville was replaced in February 1292 by the Dumfriesshire knight Sir Walter de Corry, and the Guardians of Scotland authorised the chamberlain, Henry Balliol, to pay the new keeper his annual fee.[50] In March 1292, however, the castle appears to have been in the keepership of the Nithsdale knight Sir Richard Siward.[51]

Following the English conquest of Scotland in spring/summer 1296, Edward I placed Henry Percy in possession of Wigtown and the other royal castles of the south-west and established him as warden over Ayr, Wigtown, Kircudbright and Dumfries.[52] In August 1297 Percy was replaced by John de Hoddleston.[53] Although there is no hard evidence for its fall, circumstantial evidence indicates that the castle was probably retaken by the Scots in 1297–98. Certainly, when Edward I campaigned in Galloway in the summer of 1300, the ford over the Cree was defended against him by Scots led by the Earl of Buchan and John Comyn younger of Badenoch, and was the scene of some bloody skirmishing as the English tried to force their way across to the Wigtownshire side.[54] Although the Scots were driven back at the ford, it is unclear if the English were able to extend their control west of the river, and the castle at Wigtown may have remained in Scottish hands possibly as late as their 1304 surrender to Edward I.[55] An English garrison was maintained thereafter at Wigtown. In late 1305 the castle was probably the base for Edward I's escheators in Scotland who were visiting Galloway as part of their ayre and who were escorted from Wigtown to Kirkcudbright by 20 foot-soldiers from the garrison.[56] No record survives of the capture of the castle by the supporters of Robert Bruce, but it probably fell during the Bruce campaigns in Galloway between 1308 and 1312. It appears to have been slighted following its seizure and never subsequently rebuilt.

The lines of the castle's enclosure were exposed in 1830 in a wall-chasing 'excavation' directed by Captain Robert McKerlie, father of the local antiquary Peter M'Kerlie. Long before then, however, the building had effectively disappeared as a landmark, the materials probably having been quarried for building-stone by burgesses. The excavation revealed a broad ditch on the north side, where the outer wall, following a distinctly curved course, survived to some height.[57] This high stretch of walling has since vanished and the castle remains are now heavily eroded by cattle trampling (see **fig 7**).

The Fleming Earldom of Wigtown, 1341–72

During the steady recovery of the Bruce party's position in Scotland in the period 1333–41, among the most consistently loyal of the young David II's supporters was Sir Malcolm Fleming of Cumbernauld or Lenzie, who had served as bailie of Carrick and steward of the royal household in the 1320s.[58] Although he held office in Carrick, where he enjoyed strong ties with a number of local families, and had also received some small estates in Wigtownshire from Robert I, Malcolm's primary landed interests were in lower Clydesdale and Dunbartonshire. Following David II's return from exile in France in May 1341, Malcolm was in regular attendance on the king. He had been among those lords who had met David on his landing at Inverbervie in the Mearns, and immediately assumed a position within the tight circle of royal councillors.[59] In late autumn 1341 David came to Ayr, from where raids may have been launched against the heartlands of Edward Balliol's support in Galloway.

It is probably no coincidence that it was at Ayr, where the strength of Malcolm's Carrick following was most in evidence, that David formally recognised Malcolm's loyalty through the crisis years after 1333 when in November 1341 he granted him the earldom created from the lands of the sheriffdom, with the burgh of Wigtown as his principal seat, and with rights of regality and special judicial powers to give real force to his title as earl.[60] As a consequence of this award, Wigtown ceased to be a 'royal' burgh and became the property of the earl. This development was to have damaging consequences for the burgh in the early sixteenth century during legal disputes with Whithorn over trading rights. Wigtown's royal charter would probably have been surrendered for cancellation at the time Fleming received his earldom, which meant that the town was unable subsequently to produce documentary evidence older than Whithorn's royal charters to support its case that it was a more ancient privileged community than its neighbour and had a right to a local monopoly on international trade.

Within his new earldom, Malcolm's landed base was composed of portions of the former demesne estates of King Robert I's younger brother, Edward Bruce, and Edward's illegitimate son, Alexander Bruce, Earl of Carrick, which had technically reverted to the crown in 1333 on the death of the latter at the battle of Halidon Hill. Based on fifteenth-century evidence, these estates comprised a cluster of properties in the central Machars district of Wigtownshire, mostly in the immediate hinterland south and west of Wigtown, with a scatter of outlying lands in the northern Moors area and in the Rhinns.[61] It was hardly a dominating landholding in the region and Malcolm's future domination of western Galloway probably relied on the support that he could draw from the Carrick-based men in his following, but, most importantly, on his regality jurisdiction, rather than on his limited landholding. Given the continuing support for Edward Balliol among leading western Galloway families, particularly the MacDowells, it was also a highly speculative award. In effect, Malcolm was being given parchment titles which, if he wished to turn them into a reality, he would have to pursue actively in the field: he was being given a vested interest in securing control of Galloway for the Bruce cause, and down to 1345 Malcolm was a leading figure in campaigns in the region.

There is little evidence that Earl Malcolm was a regular resident in either his earldom or its 'chief place', his principal base remaining the great royal castle of Dumbarton, of which he was the keeper. There is no record of how he administered Wigtown, and only a few indications that he sought to exercise leadership in the region.[62] The king's ability to extract additional taxation from Wigtownshire, however, does appear to have been enhanced in the later 1350s, probably following Earl Malcolm's death in c 1358 which saw subsequent crown intrusion into an area where strong local lordship was thus weakened. In the 'contribution' (a tax for the king's support) of 1358, for example, Wigtownshire paid £57, which compares well with the combined £92 from Cunningham and Kyle, or £73 from Stirlingshire.[63] The long absence of Malcolm's grandson and successor, Thomas Fleming, 2nd Earl of Wigtown, as one of the hostages in England for the payment of David II's ransom after 1357, probably saw further erosion of any influence the 1st Earl had built up. There is no evidence for any closeness between the king and the new earl to match that between David and Earl Malcolm.

Thomas's prolonged stay in England meant that there was no formal infeftment of the new earl, and Wigtown probably lay in royal hands for several years after 1358 and, possibly, after Thomas's return to Scotland in 1363. The king could not prevent Thomas from inheriting the earldom altogether, as it had been granted in entail, but he could alter the terms by which it was held. In January 1366/67 Thomas finally had a re-grant of the earldom of Wigtown as held by his grandfather, but shorn of regality powers.[64] The clawing-back of such jurisdictions was a feature of royal policy in the 1360s, most notably by the Act of Revocation of September 1367, but David was prepared to grant specific exemptions, as in Moray, where such powers were essential for the maintenance of law and order.

The king can have had few illusions as to the likely consequence of the loss of these powers in Wigtown, for Thomas possessed no greater landed base in the earldom than his grandfather, and did not enjoy the same intimacy with the south Ayrshire nobility which had reinforced Malcolm's authority in the 1340s. Thomas was earl in title, but the loss of regality fatally undermined his ability to exercise lordship in his earldom, and he was soon facing considerable local opposition. This came both from native families, again headed by the MacDowells, whom David had restored to something of their former powers, and from the Kennedys. Always lukewarm in their support for Malcolm, they were now firmly aligned with Robert Stewart, the king's nephew and heir-presumptive, and were steadily expanding their influence south from Carrick.

Further local difficulties were stirred up for Thomas by his new neighbour to the east, Archibald Douglas 'the Grim', David's principal henchman, who had been given the lands between the Rivers Cree and Nith, the eastern portion of the old lordship of Galloway, and the title of Lord of Galloway.[65] David's death in 1371 did not lift this pressure from Thomas, for the new king, Robert Stewart, now openly pursued his aggressive dismantling of the Fleming lordship. Eventually, burdened by debts and unable to impose his lordship over the greater vassals of his earldom, Thomas resigned it to the crown and, on 19 April 1372, resigned it formally a second time into the hands of Robert II.[66]

The following day, King Robert made a grant of the 'whole lordship of Wigtown, together with the burgh of the same, excepting the barony of Carnsmoel [Kirkinner]' to 'his dearest nephew', Sir James Lindsay.[67] Lindsay was not granted the title of earl, but received the whole lordship and power of regality over it. Robert II clearly understood the requirements for strong lordship in this notoriously turbulent zone. Lindsay, however, was unable to effect possession, as by this time physical control of Wigtown had been assumed by Archibald Douglas. Douglas was a man whom even the new king, with whom he had clashed politically, could ill afford to challenge. His power rested on a formidable military following backed by the substantial landed inheritance of his wife. He was thus in a position to offer the lordship which Thomas had failed to provide, and may in fact have been encouraged by David in efforts to undermine the earl. It emerged that continuing financial embarrassment and bitter disputes with local noblemen had led Thomas in February 1371/72 – two months before his nominal surrender of the same lands to the crown – to sell the earldom to Archibald. King Robert was forced to accept the dubious legality of this transaction and confirmed Archibald in possession of Wigtown but withheld the title of earl, which was later to form a cause célèbre in the conflict between James II and Archibald's Black Douglas descendants. Kennedy ambitions in Wigtown had also been checked by Douglas's coup, but at the cost of decades of simmering rivalry between the two families.

The Douglas Earldom, 1372–1455

The establishment of a single lordship encompassing the whole of Galloway and controlled by the Douglas family provided the strong regional leadership which had been lacking, especially in Wigtownshire, since the 1350s. In the last quarter of the fourteenth century, Archibald stamped his mark firmly on the region, curbing the power of the greater native families and introducing his own kin and dependants as landholders.[68] The burgh itself remained firmly under Douglas domination. As Archibald's power grew, however, especially after his succession to the earldom of Douglas in 1388, his direct connection with western Galloway probably diminished significantly. Wigtown appears to have become little more than a regional backwater, nominally managed but in reality largely neglected by the Douglases, and significant only as an outlet for the produce of their south-western estates and as a meeting-place for the head court of the earldom.[69]

After 1372 the title Earl of Wigtown appears to have lain dormant until 1419, when it was revived for Archibald 4th Earl of Douglas's eldest son and heir, Archibald.[70] There was, however, no formal royal award of the title and, more significantly, when the 4th Earl returned to war in France in 1424, leaving his eldest son as his deputy in Scotland, control of Galloway was not vested in him but in his mother, Margaret Stewart, daughter of Robert III. This separation of title from real power was compounded after his father's death in 1424, for in 1426 King James I formalised his sister's possession of Galloway with a royal charter granting her possession for life.[71] It may have been that the king was using this grant as a device to separate Wigtown from Douglas control, and it was fortunate for the earl that both he and his mother outlived James.

Archibald, now 5th Earl of Douglas, was forced to make his own mark on the region in a series of demonstrations of his personal power and status to the local nobility.[72] This included compearing at what were probably formal meetings of the head court of the earldom at Wigtown, for example, on 3 April 1432, when he confirmed his mother's own 1430 confirmation of a whole series of grants in favour of the monks of Glenluce Abbey.[73] As the witness lists to such confirmations demonstrate, the gathering of the court was a major social occasion at which the greater and lesser landholders of western Galloway, lay and ecclesiastical, could assemble. The dates of the courts coincided with the Easter and Martinmas quarter-days, which may also have been the dates for two of the burgh's annual fairs, thereby combining social gathering with commerce.[74] There could perhaps have been no better occasions for Earl Archibald to impress his power on the people.

The traumatic coups within the Douglas family in 1440, which included the judicial murders of Archibald's sons, William, 6th Earl of Douglas, and David, Master of Douglas, at the instigation of their great-uncle, James the Gross, 1st Earl of Avondale, saw the beginnings of a breach between the people of Galloway and the heads of the Douglas line. James the Gross, as 7th Earl of Douglas, strove to secure control of all the portions of the inheritance, arranging for the marriage of the 5th earl's remaining child, Margaret, to his eldest son, William. In c 1447, William, by then 8th Earl of Douglas, secured the resignation of Galloway in his favour by the aged Countess Margaret, his wife's grandmother.[75] This resignation was formally recognised by the king in 1450, perhaps in return for Douglas support for the royal attack in that year on the Livingston family.

Earl William, it appeared, was benefiting from a close relationship with the crown and future strengthening of his position seemed likely. However, in 1451, while the earl was absent on pilgrimage to Rome for the papal jubilee, King James began a deliberate assault on Douglas power. Despite the confirmation of 1450, Galloway was the principal target, a change of mind possibly triggered by the death of Countess Margaret.[76] For the king, the seizure of land to which Douglas title was dubious offered an opportunity to secure income that was needed to fulfil his obligations to provide adequate dower lands for his wife, Mary of Gueldres. King James, however, had misjudged the situation and by June a compromise settlement was proposed with the earl, who had by then reached England. This provided for the return to the earl of all of his lands with the exception only of the earldom of Wigtown and the lordship of Stewarton in Renfrewshire.

Circumstances elsewhere in the kingdom, however, soon forced the king to compromise over those two properties also. Mounting tension in the north of the kingdom in the summer of 1451 drove the king to turn to the Douglases, who held extensive lordships in Moray and Easter Ross, for support against the MacDonalds. In return, King James was forced to recognise Douglas rights to the earldom of Wigtown. Accordingly, on 26 October 1451, following the empty show of Earl William's formal resignation of the earldom into the king's hands in parliament, James 'restored' it to him, but this time with clearly defined rights of lordship and possession which removed the question-mark which had hung over Douglas tenure of Wigtown since the time of Archibald the Grim.[77] William now held the earldom in free regality, controlling also 'the tower' and burgh of Wigtown, where he had the right to have the tron and to uplift great and little customs, as well as to hold the royal justiciary and chamberlain ayres in the burgh. For this enhanced position, the earl was burdened with the blench ferme payment of one red rose at Wigtown on the feast of the birth of St John the Baptist (24 June).

Once confirmed in possession of Wigtown, Earl William appears to have begun immediate action against those local lairds who had displayed disloyalty to him in favour of the king. Among his casualties may have been the Agnews, who had been associated particularly with Countess Margaret's administration in the 1440s. Such actions served in the long term to weaken further the reserves of support in Galloway which had been built up by Archibald the Grim in the later fourteenth century. The strained relationship between James II and Earl William climaxed in the king's hot-blooded murder of the earl at Stirling in 1453. Unprepared for the consequences of his actions, the king quickly reached a settlement with William's younger brother, James, who was confirmed as 9th Earl of Douglas. In 1455, however, the king was ready to move against the Black Douglases and, although Threave Castle in the Stewartry proved to be the last Douglas stronghold to hold out against the royal forces, the extent to which Douglas control over Galloway had slipped away since 1440 was revealed by the number of local families who abandoned their nominal overlords and sided with King James. Douglas power collapsed spectacularly in the face of a swift royal campaign, reinforced by formal acts of forfeiture in parliament laid against the Earl of Douglas and his brothers.

The late fifteenth-century burgh

Following the forfeiture of James, 9th Earl of Douglas, in 1455, Galloway and its two chief burghs passed into direct royal lordship once more. In 1457, James II issued a reconfirmation of Wigtown's old privileges as a royal burgh, possibly using the model of an early fourteenth-century charter of Robert I.[78]

The charter confirmed the burgesses' rights in Wigtown itself plus the adjacent lands of Borrowmoss, Culquhirk, Broadfield, Clauchrie, Kirvennie and Philipland, the burgh commons, mill (the earliest specific reference to a burgh mill) and fishings. The sphere of immediate control around the burgh was implicitly defined by the Bishop Burn to the north, the Bladnoch to the south, the Cree estuary to the east, and the lordship of Torhouse, possessed by the MacDowell family, to the west. Its economic hinterland, however, embraced the whole district from 'le mydstreme' of the River Cree on the east to the sea of Ireland on the west, an ill-defined description which was later to bring the burgesses into collision with their Whithorn neighbours. Although it had been restored to the status of a royal burgh, Wigtown continued to be treated as a disposable item in the royal portfolio. In 1473, for example, as part of the marriage settlement for Margaret of Denmark out of the crown lands, James III granted his wife the royal properties and rights in Galloway on both sides of the Cree, together with the customs and burgage fermes of both Kirkcudbright and Wigtown.[79] The burgh evidently mattered little to its royal superiors, so it came to be dominated by the politically ambitious families of the region.

It is in the second half of the fifteenth century that a clearer picture emerges of the leading members of the burgess community and the interconnectedness of the burgh with the leading landed families of Galloway. Among the principal families of the burgh were the Murdochsons, the McGarvies and the Makcristens or McCristens, several generations of the last holding key offices in Wigtown. The McGarvie family, among whose number was the ambitious and influential William, later parson of Wigtown, possessed a tenement on the south of the burgh, in what is now South Main Street, flanked by two properties owned by the Murdochsons.[80] This tenement, lying on what seems to have been the less highly regarded side of the street (though it may not have been the McGarvies' main holding), was given in 1474 to William, already described as 'Mr' (meaning a university graduate and cleric). The legal transaction was witnessed by a number of burgesses and local lairds, including the influential Uhtred McDowell of Logan, head of one of the most powerful branches of that family, his presence underscoring the connections enjoyed by the McGarvies.

The McCristens were an acquisitive family who sought not only to expand their holdings in the burgh in the late fifteenth century, but also to retain possession of their gains.[81] The head of the family, John McCristen, had been provost in 1459 and, by the time he again held that office in 1470–71, his family had moved from the ranks of the burgesses into the minor landholding gentry.[82] Their main residence by that date lay just north of the burgh at Monkhill. In 1484, John Makcristen resigned the lands of Monkhill into the hands of the provost and baillies, for them to re-grant the property immediately to his son Simon.[83] Simon McCristen possessed at least two tenements in Wigtown, one on the north and one on the south of the main street, and at least one croft on its north side. Monkhill, however, while remaining an element of the burgh's lands and held from the burgesses at feu, formed the core of his estates, to which by the end of the century he had added Kilsture and Claunch in Sorbie parish to the south as well as Carseriggan.[84] Simon was clearly a power in the community, and as early as 1497 served as bailie of Wigtown.[85] In the early 1500s, his dominance of the burgh was to result in litigation and accusations of oppression and illegal trading.[86]

Of all the individuals who figure in the late medieval history of Wigtown perhaps the most unsavoury is Rankin Mure. His career has been discussed in detail elsewhere and will only be summarised here.[87] A younger son of an already powerful local family, he emerged first as a manager of property on behalf of others, and quickly established himself as a financier and mortgager. Sharp business practice more than once threatened to ruin him. It brought lawsuits but also physical possession of properties in Wigtown and its hinterland in the 1480s and 1490s. Property acquired as security on defaulted loans to minor local lairds made him a man of substance in the burgh, and it was possibly as a result of this standing that his son, Patrick, came to hold the office of alderman by 1506, and subsequently the provostship on five separate occasions. Where the McCristens moved from the ranks of the burgesses into that of the regional landholding class, the Mures moved deliberately in the other direction, retaining their landholding status while securing influence within the burgh. In this they symbolised one of the key trends in the later medieval and early modern history of Wigtown, where local landholders sought to gain property within the burgh and through that to win political influence which would give them an edge in the continually shifting regional power-politics.

There were other prominent families from outside Wigtown who contended with the McCristens and Mures for influence in the burgh. Among them were the Murrays of Broughton, who were building up a landholding on either side of the Cree estuary, and establishing junior members in the principal burghs of the region. One John Murray was a burgess of Kirkcudbright and his illegitimate son, William, had secured property in Wigtown by the mid-1400s. On William Murray's death in 1473, his tenement and garden in the burgh fell to the crown by reason of his bastardy, whereupon James III granted them to Sir John Carlisle of Torthorwald in Dumfriesshire, introducing a further important regional family into the local power-structure. Around the same time, other families from the east of Galloway, principally the Maclellans and McKies from the Kirkcudbright and Glenkens districts, were establishing interests in Wigtown. Together with Wigtownshire families like the Ahannays and McDowells, these important kindreds were to exert powerful influences over the political and economic life of the burgh down to the seventeenth century. In the late 1400s, however, it was chiefly a succession of ambitious and unscrupulous men like Simon McCristen or Rankin Mure who dominated the town.

Religious life

Wigtown is one of several medieval Scottish burghs (for example Cupar, Dunbar, Haddington and Roxburgh) where the original parish church lay outside the town. Almost certainly, as was the case with Cupar, the foundation of the church pre-dated the development of the settlement, and the dedication of the church to the otherwise-obscure seventh-century Welsh/Breton saint, Machutus (St Malo), and the discovery of part of a cross-slab of probably tenth-century date in the medieval cemetery, might point to very early origins (**fig 10**).[88]

It is likely that in the twelfth and earlier thirteenth centuries the patronage of the church lay in the hands of the Lords of Galloway and that it remained a free parsonage with all fruits enjoyed by the parsons or rectors.[89] Following the death of Alan of Galloway, the right of presentation may have fallen to his youngest daughter, Dervorgilla, who certainly had a landed interest in Wigtown later in the century.[90] Following the defeat and deposition of her son, King John, in 1296, the rights and properties of the Balliol family in Scotland were assumed by Edward I of England along with the Scottish crown lands. It was thus to Edward II in 1308 that the monks of Sweetheart Abbey appealed for a grant of the church of Wigtown to help make good the financial losses which they had suffered as a result of the actions of English

FIGURE 10
The ruins of the medieval and post-Reformation church (Martin Brann)

officials.[91] If the grant was made, it does not appear to have been effective, and Sweetheart was never to secure possession. Although the English grip on Galloway had been broken by 1313 and English garrisons expelled from Scotland altogether by 1318, as late as *c* 1319 English royal clerks still sought presentation to Scottish benefices as a reward for their service. In 1319, Thomas de Cotyngham, clerk of Edward II's chancery, petitioned for – and received – the church of Wigtown.[92] It is unlikely that he ever secured possession, for before that date Edward Bruce, to whom King Robert had given the lordship of Galloway, had granted the church to the canons of Whithorn.[93] That grant, however, seems only to have been of the right of presentation and the canons were never able to secure full control of its revenues, despite a number of attempts.[94] At the time of the Reformation, Wigtown was one of the few remaining free parsonages in Scotland.

It is unsurprising that families already influential in local secular politics should also seek to dominate the ecclesiastical life of the community. In the late 1400s it was the McGarvies who appear most active. On 8 August 1495 the rising cleric Master William McGarvie endowed a chaplainry at the altar of the Blessed Virgin Mary and St Ninian, described as located in a chapel on the south side of the parish church, making over to it two tenements and two crofts he possessed in the burgh.[95] The chaplain was to hold the property for his lifetime, and after his death it was to fall to the alderman and baillies of the burgh to provide the new chaplain. It was a generous endowment and the three chaplains who were among the witnesses to his charter may have been hopeful of benefiting from it. A chaplainry of St Michael the Archangel was also founded in the parish church by William McGarvie at an unrecorded date. In 1490, McGarvie was still not in possession of an ecclesiastical benefice, despite his university education and position as a notary public. By 1495, however, he held the rich vicarage of Penninghame, the parish immediately to the north of Wigtown, which was in the gift of the Bishop of Whithorn, and by 1506 he also held the office of commissary of Farines.[96] He was clearly well connected locally, as the witnesses to his charter of 1495 testify. All were influential men: Patrick McKie of Cumloden, Uhtred McDowell of Mindork, the infamous Rankin Mure, and Norman McCulloch of Torhouse. It is possible that McGarvie hoped to use these connections to secure the rich parsonage of Wigtown as his next step on the ladder, but there is no record that he was successful. Instead, for most of the period *c* 1475 to the Reformation in 1560, the parsonage of Wigtown was held by members of the Vaus or Vans of Barnbarroch, one of the most influential landholding families in Wigtownshire.[97] Connections were all very well, but blood ties mattered more.

In common with most pre-Reformation parish churches in Scotland, that at Wigtown fulfilled as great a secular role as a spiritual one. The high altars of parish churches were, for example, often designated as the place for the paying of a debt or the redeeming of a mortgage. In 1488, the high altar was where the local property speculator, Rankin Mure, undertook to restore Henry Mundwell to lands in the Stewartry in return for a payment of £40 Scots. In 1541 it was where Patrick Maclellan of Gelston would restore possession of the right to uplift certain rents to Fergus McDowell of Freugh for the payment of 200 merks Scots.[98] Even after the Reformation such traditional practices persisted despite the hostility of the new Church authorities, and in 1576 the church was the named venue for a reversion payment in a property deal between John Dunbar of Mochrum and his nephew.[99] Actual legal business was also transacted in the church. In 1522, for example, it was the location for the beginning of an action before the commissary of Whithorn, John McCracken, concerning church property.[100]

As is the case with most of the smaller communities of the various mendicant orders in Scotland, the history of the Dominican convent in Wigtown is quite obscure, and even the exact location of the building is uncertain, as discussed in detail above. The friary is said to have been founded *c* 1267 by Dervorgilla, daughter of Alan of Galloway and wife of John Balliol I of Barnard Castle, but the sole authority for this claim is the early fifteenth-century chronicler Andrew of Wyntoun.[101] The first surviving contemporary reference to the friary occurs only in 1297 when the English administration in Scotland authorised payment from the fermes of the Scottish burghs to various Dominican houses.[102]

One prior of Wigtown, Ninian Shanks, served as principal of the order in Scotland in the late 1490s,[103] but this does not mean that the convent was particularly large or influential. Indeed, the revenues of the friary appear always to have been slight and were supplemented frequently by royal almsgiving. The exchequer accounts for 1327–28 of Henry, son of Michael, former provost of the burgh, record payments of 16 merks per annum to the prior and convent, and of £4 per annum each 'of the king's alms' to Brothers John of Man and Patrick McEwen, who both seem to have been Dominicans. The first payment appears to have been a long-standing grant to the convent from the burgh rents, possibly dating from the time of King Alexander II, but the two latter were apparently specific gifts made by Robert I. The same year, Patrick McEwen, provost, accounted for royal alms payments of £26 13s 4d to the friars, the increased figure probably reflecting a death-bed bequest of the late king.[104]

Irregular payments of alms to the friars of Wigtown occur in the reign of James IV and reflect the king's residence in the town during his pilgrimages to Whithorn. Most occurred on his return journey, starting in August 1501 with a gift of 28s.[105] He was there again in April 1503, when another 28s was given, and it was while there that news was brought to him of the death of his infant son, the Earl of Mar, for which another 40s was given 'to the Freris and preistis to do dirige and saule mes'.[106] From September 1504 until July

1507, each visit was marked by an alms payment of 14s,[107] with additional individual payments, such as that in May 1506 'to the freir of Wigtoun that suld haf singin his first mes the next Sonday'.[108] James may have resided at the convent during his visits to the burgh, as payments of 28s in 1506 and 14s in 1507 for 'belcheir' there are recorded.[109] The 1507 account, however, distinguishes between 28s given for belcheir 'quhar the king lay' and 14s for belcheir to the friars 'quhar the king dynyt',[110] which suggests that although he may have dined with the prior and brethren he lodged elsewhere.

Among the more valuable of the friars' interests was the salmon fishing on the south side of the Bladnoch which had been granted to them by the crown, perhaps as early as the thirteenth century. In 1526, James V gave them a 13-year lease of the remaining crown salmon-fishing on the north side of the river, which in 1541 was converted into a gift in free alms, the stipulated service being that the 'priour and freiris and thair successouris singand daily eftir evinsang in thair place of Wigtoun *Salve Regina* with ane speciale orisone' for King James IV and Queen Margaret.[111] A broader indication of the extent of the Dominicans' lands and income from around Wigtown is obtained only at the end of the convent's life. Contrary to the often-stated view that the friary revenues were probably made over to the burgh at the time of the Reformation, the beneficiary was one of the most influential local families.[112] On 21 December 1560 the prior and brethren feued what appears to have been all their properties and rents to Sir Alexander Stewart of Garlies, his wife, and their male heirs.[113]

The cemetery of the friary appears to have functioned as a meeting-place for the settling of legal business. The consecrated ground upon which the business was transacted gave added weight to the undertakings. In June 1525, the burial-ground was the scene of a confrontation between William Lennox of Cally and John Mccrecken (or McCracken), commissary of Wigtown, who had condemned Lennox for some unspecified transgression.[114] This role, however, appears to have disappeared with the Reformation.

Traditions of a chapel of St John derive from references to a 'St John's land' near the burgh.[115] This, however, seems simply to have been one of the numerous small parcels of land from which the Knights of St John of Jerusalem (the Hospitallers) drew rents. Their lands at Wigtown were recorded in 1539–40 as yielding an annual rent of 4 shillings.[116] After the Reformation St John's Land found its way into secular hands, separated from the secularised Lordship of St John, and in the early seventeenth century belonged to the Ahannays. In 1629 it was described as lying outwith the east end of the burgh.[117]

In addition to the parish church and its two associated chaplainries, there appears to have been a separate chapel within the burgh lands. The only reference occurs in August 1581, when 'the lane leading to the chapel of St Bride' was given as one of the boundaries of a property in an instrument of sasine.[118] Other than the probability that this chapel lay on the northern side of the burgh, there is no precise indication of it location. Suggestions that a further chapel lay at Kilquhirn on the south-west of the burgh are based on the assumption that the *kil-* prefix derived from the Gaelic *cille*, a church. The earliest recorded forms of this name, however, are *Kerquhorne* or *Kirriquhirne*, the prefix clearly derived from the Gaelic *ceathramh*, meaning a quarter-land.[119]

The burgh's trade *c* 1400–*c* 1600

The precinct falling under the supervision of the joint custumars of Wigtown and Whithorn in 1535 embraced 'the burrowis of Wigtoun and Quhithirne and all the boundis and fredomes therof and all uthiris boundis betuix Glennop and the watter of Cre and the west sey cost of the oceane sey and Lochryane and the Rynnis of Galloway'.[120] It is likely that this precinct had the same bounds as had been set down for the burgh's jurisdiction in the thirteenth century. Surviving reference to a custumar of Wigtown dates only from 1330, when Henry the Clerk, collector of the 'new custom', accounted for 18s 4d to the exchequer.[121] For the following year he accounted for 41s 8d.[122] Between 1476 and 1503, and for short periods thereafter, the custumar of Kirkcudbright held a joint authority over Kirkcudbright and Wigtown.[123] After 1505, the custumars were usually tacksmen who paid an agreed annual duty to the crown and retained any surplus receipts for themselves. In the early 1500s, the customs tacksman for Wigtown and Whithorn was the influential local laird Mungo Murray of Broughton, whose grandson and heir, John Murray, was liable for payment of the balance of Mungo's tack due at the exchequer up to the date of grandfather's death in April 1515.[124]

The bulk of the customable goods leaving Galloway in the Middle Ages appears to have consisted of wool, hides and woollen cloth, with Kirkcudbright being the chief burgh trading in these commodities. In 1434 over 71 sacks of wool were exported through that port,[125] but its trade collapsed in 1455,[126] perhaps partly as a consequence of the overthrow of the Black Douglas family in that year. The Douglases, as Lords of Galloway and Earls of Wigtown, had controlled both Kirkcudbright and Wigtown but, although wool was also being produced in western Galloway, appear to have concentrated collection and export through Kirkcudbright, which lay closest to their regional power-base at Threave Castle. Wider economic factors may also have contributed to the decline in the Galloway wool trade, for there was no recovery in export levels in the later fifteenth or early sixteenth centuries,[127] although by 1510–11 the Isle of Whithorn had emerged as an alternative port. One key factor may have been the development of trade in woollen cloth rather than raw wool. In 1459, the custumar of Kirkcudbright accounted for 1440 ells of cloth, rising to 3600 ells by 1511.[128] By the same date Wigtown was accounting for 1660 ells and Whithorn 2560 ells,[129] figures which underline both the prior of

Whithorn's reasons for securing confirmation of his burgh's trading privileges from James IV, and the efforts by the burgesses of Wigtown to halt their local rival's growth.

The importance of cattle in the economy of medieval Galloway is emphasised by the volume of hides exported. In 1434, 1330 hides were exported through Kirkcudbright, a figure which perhaps represents a total for the entire region,[130] although in 1477–78 1000 were shipped from there, while 1250 were exported through Wigtown.[131] As with woollen cloth, by 1511 Wigtown had lost the bulk of the western Galloway trade in hides to Whithorn, which was exporting 510 as against 220 through Wigtown.[132] Indeed, by that date Whithorn was the chief export centre for hides in Galloway, its total almost equalling the combined figures for Wigtown and Kirkcudbright.

Even at peak periods of trading activity, the volume of goods passing through the port at Wigtown represented only a tiny proportion of national exports and probably the activities of only one or two ships, though it was a significant enough port to appear in the earliest surviving Scottish navigational guide.[133] At Kirkcudbright, the highest customs payments, collected in 1434–35, were the yield of five vessels, and the average of two ships per annum recorded there or at Wigtown in 1487–89 and 1500–01 probably represents the more usual level of trade in the later fifteenth and early sixteenth centuries.[134] Avoidance of tolls and customs, however, may account for some of the apparently low level of trade, as is suggested by claims that Breton, French and Irish vessels were coming into unofficial harbours in the Rhinns in the 1520s with the connivance of certain Wigtown burgesses, who were also illegally uplifting the customs on the cargoes.[135]

The bulk of the goods coming into Wigtown in the late medieval period appear to have been wine, salt and other provisions. Most of the long-distance trade seems to have been from the Biscay region of western France and northern Spain. It was probably from there that the ship which was the subject of a case before the Lords Auditors in October 1483 came. This involved a complaint by one 'Johne Tapy merchaint of Spanze' against 'Bertilmow Carnis and Oliver Laboddo maister of a schip callit ye Mary of Guerrande'. Tapy was claiming for payment of 405 crowns for 15 tuns of wine bought from him by Carnis and insured by Laboddo for carrying to Wigtown. Tapy produced a charter-party in court containing various clauses safeguarding him against losses caused by leakage or by the crew drinking the cargo.[136] Further evidence for a western-French trading connection comes from reference in 1512 to a vessel, the St Marie de Biscay, which was unloaded at Whithorn and Wigtown, presumably of a cargo of wine and Biscay salt.[137] Wine was also the main cargo imported in 1527 by the Breton Jean Chevalier, merchant of St Malo.[138] For his cargo of 18 tuns of Gascon wine, the council paid 24 crowns per tun and 22d for the ship's entry into the haven, two-thirds of the price to be paid as 'penworttis' (the equivalent value in other goods) and the remaining third in silver. Two Wigtown burgesses appear to have acted as middlemen and delivered Chevalier notice of the offer, which included free passage and permission to sell the wine in 'the greit skayre' (the great market square), the first surviving reference to the main market area of the burgh. A third cargo of wine was recorded in February 1531/32 – a ship with 20 tuns of wine from La Rochelle and 120 bolls of Biscay salt.[139]

The impact of the great domestic upheavals of the mid-sixteenth century on the trading life of the kingdom has tended to be overshadowed by the political and religious aspects. At a time when communication with foreign parts could be viewed with suspicion, merchants needed to act with circumspection and secure licences to travel abroad. In January 1560, eight Wigtown merchants secured such a permit under a bond of surety for £1000 Scots by Sir John Gordon of Lochinvar.[140] Described as 'true and obedient servants of the crown', they were allowed to go on their business to France and return with their goods to Wigtown, but were not to traffic their goods with any rebels.

The dispute with Whithorn

The burgesses of neighbouring Whithorn were given additional mercantile rights by James IV in the 1490s, and seem to have extended their trading operations to a point where they began to have a significant impact on Wigtown's trade. Wigtown launched an action before the Lords of Council in 1510 intended to halt this trade, which it claimed was contrary to its privileges and rights.[141] The case was continued until 1511. The burgesses of Wigtown protested to the Lords of Council that the ratification of the charters 'should not turn them nor their freedoms to prejudice'.[142] Their argument was based on the fundamental assumption that as the older, and unequivocally royal, burgh, their rights took precedence over those of Whithorn.

However, the weakness of Wigtown's case was that although it had held royal burgh status since the mid-thirteenth century, it could not produce parchment evidence. Prior Henry of Whithorn in 1512 offered to show his priory's records to the court and demonstrate that they were older than anything held by Wigtown.[143] In 1518, however, Wigtown displayed its royal charter, dating from 1457,[144] and, although that had seemed sufficient to establish Wigtown's right, it was actually from that point that its case began to unravel. Although the Lords of Council found against Whithorn on the strength of the 1457 charter, the record of the court's decision was later formally cancelled. In March 1519 Whithorn asked for a formal registration of the date of Wigtown's charter, which post-dated their own charter from Robert I.[145] Wigtown all but recognised that the case was lost and had begun to negotiate for a compromise some days earlier; the case records then fall silent.

The sixteenth-century burgh

The emergence of political factionalism in Wigtown in the closing decades of the fifteenth century was but a foretaste of the struggles which followed in the sixteenth century. The tightness of the group of men who made up the political community and their physical relationships in the close confines of the town facilitated close co-operation but also enhanced the potential for conflict. Facing the great square in the vicinity of the market cross (then probably at the east end, near the tolbooth) was apparently the most prestigious area of the town, the location of some of the finest houses of burgesses and town-houses of the leading local lairds. Among these were the Agnews of Lochnaw, hereditary sheriffs of Wigtown, who may only have acquired a private residence in the burgh in the early 1510s. This property came by crown grant following its seizure on grounds of the bastardy of its former holder, John MakMurrawe or Wrycht, in 1511.[146] The naming of four Agnews, including Sir Matthew, the sheriff, as defenders in an action raised by John Vaus, parson of Wigtown, in 1524, concerning a property dispute in the burgh, however, suggests that the family was already well established there.[147] Also from the 1510s comes the first firm evidence for the possession of property in the burgh by the Maclellans of Bombie. In 1516, an instrument of sasine referred to land held by the Laird of Bombie on the north side of the burgh.[148] A third influential family was the MacCullochs of Torhouse, who held property in the burgh before 1513.[149]

By 1549, another site on the north side of the 'Hie Gait' (North Main Street) 'fornentis the Mercate Croce' was possessed by William Ahannay, who was provost between 1551 and 1554.[150] In 1549, Ahannay received permission to 'rais and sett furth the heid of his hous … with battaling and corbel sailze in the maist honest and substantious maner he pleisis and sall think maist expedient'. This seems to have been one of the most substantial properties in the burgh and its finishing in this manner may have been an explicit recognition of the local dominance of the Ahannay family, which had provided the town with its provosts since at least 1536.[151] The apparent naming of the vennel at the east end of the north side of the main street in the late seventeenth century as 'hannayes' may point to the siting of this substantial property almost directly opposite the tolbooth.[152] Although there had presumably been some form of tolbooth or council-meeting building in the burgh in the medieval period, it is not until 1587 that one is mentioned in surviving records, on which occasion it served as the venue for a session of the burgh court.[153]

Indications of conflict between rival groups jockeying for influence in the burgh emerges early in the sixteenth century. In October 1507, Patrick Dunbar, heir of Patrick Dunbar of Kilconquhar, and two others, received a remission from James IV for their part in the slaughter of Patrick McCulloch in Wigtown. The Dunbars, headed by the Mochrum branch of the family, and the McCullochs, led by the Laird of Myrton, were two of the leading kindreds of the Machars.

This incident seems to have been part of a struggle for local influence. Of wider regional significance was the attempted intrusion of influence by families from outwith the shire. Mention has already been made of the Maclellans of Bombie, but the most significant development in the first half of the sixteenth century was the attempted extension of power into western Galloway by the Gordons of Lochinvar, a move which was resisted by the Ahannay, Stewart of Garlies, and Vaus families. One flash-point was the rival interests of the Gordons and Stewarts in the lands of Glenluce Abbey, with which the Stewarts had been intromitting since at least the early 1500s and which the Gordons sought to secure in 1524.[154] The situation was compounded in the 1530s when the Kennedys began to spread their interests south from Carrick into Wigtownshire, again casting covetous eyes on the Glenluce estate. By the 1540s, both the Gordons and the Kennedys were contending for physical possession of the monastery and its properties, a dispute which would drag on for over two decades.[155]

By the 1590s, the struggle for regional domination had degenerated into feud and violence, with much of the struggle fought out around Wigtown. Sir Alexander Stewart of Garlies, provost of the burgh, was deeply involved in the conflict, and in 1591 was obliged to find surety of 2000 merks in his private landholding capacity and a further £1000 as provost, that he would keep the peace, following an action before the Privy Council by James Kennedy, son of John Kennedy of Blairquhan, and that he would cease to trouble Kennedy's tenants around Cruggleton, Portyerrock and Whitehills, east of Whithorn.[156] Sir Alexander's cautioners were two of his closest local allies, Alexander Ahannay of Sorbie and Gavin Dunbar of Baldoon. Court actions such as this may have prevented the violence from escalating out of control, but in the early seventeenth century local rivalries were to erupt into bloodshed.

The seventeenth-century burgh

The battle for political influence in Wigtown reached a climax at the beginning of the seventeenth century with the murder at the Cruives of Cree in December 1600 of Sir Alexander Stewart's associate and successor as provost, Patrick Ahannay of Kirkdale, at the hands of John Kennedy the younger of Blairquhan (Ayrshire).[157] The hostility between the Ahannays, Stewarts and Vaus on one side and the Kennedys on the other was well known to the Edinburgh authorities and strong efforts were made to arrest John Kennedy and bring a judicial end to the conflict.[158] With the support of his kin, however, Kennedy, although put to the horn and denounced as an outlaw and rebel, was able to avoid detention. The rival parties seem, however, to have been equally disinclined to end the matter peaceably, for in June 1601 the Privy Council sought to force both sides to give each other mutual assurances of goodwill or face sentence of outlawry.[159] The conflict, however, seems if anything to have escalated.

At around the same time as the conflict with the Kennedys was coming to a head, the Gordons mounted an attack on Stewart and his allies in the heart of their own territory in the Machars. In May 1600, Sir Robert Gordon, heir to Gordon of Lochinvar, and his local ally William McCulloch of Myrton, had bound themselves under the surety of £10,000 to keep the peace. Within weeks they attacked Sir John Vaus in his house of Barnbarroch, and then waylaid and murdered George Stewart of Dunduff on the road between Wigtown and the Clary.[160] Sir Robert and his friends had been widely regarded as threats to the peace and stability of the region and his father had been required to stand surety for his heir's good behaviour under a bond of £10,000 Scots. His failure to do so resulted in the Privy Council requiring payment,[161] which drove the Gordons deeply into debt and further fuelled their need to secure regional political influence to solve their financial woes. It was only concerted Privy Council action which finally ended the cycle of violence in the region.

There were also a number of actions brought by complainants before the Privy Council involving incidents in and around the burgh. In November 1608, what seems to have been the souring of a business relationship between an Edinburgh merchant, Nicoll Forsyth, and William M'Kie of Kirriquhirn, one of the bailies, and William Mure, was claimed by Forsyth to have ended with M'Kie pursuing him through the streets of Wigtown with a drawn sword and Mure shooting him in the shoulder with 'ane putrynell'.[162] Debts seemed to have lain behind the dispute, for in 1618 Forsyth secured the apprising of half of the property of William Mure's son for over 3400 merks owed to him by Mure.[163]

What the protracted struggles for control of the burgh seem to indicate is that in the later sixteenth and earlier seventeenth century Wigtown was worth fighting over. Its regional pre-eminence in the later sixteenth century was reinforced when it became the seat of the commissariot court for Galloway, replacing the pre-Reformation consistory court of the bishops at Whithorn; this had perhaps helped to secure its prosperity.[164] Its central place in the regional ecclesiastical structure had been further reinforced in 1588 when it was named as the venue for meetings of the local presbytery, again displacing the pre-Reformation centre at Whithorn. Even after the revival of an episcopal structure for the Scottish Church and the consecration of a new bishop at Whithorn in 1605, Wigtown remained the meeting-place for the diocesan courts, and preserved this role through the succeeding changes in Scottish church government in 1638, 1660 and 1689. Perhaps some indication of the comparative prosperity of the community in this period is the bell which survives in the present Town House, and presumably once hung in the tolbooth. Bought from Deventer in Holland, it is inscribed 'O GOD LET WIGTOUNE FLOURISH BY THY WORD IN CHRIST WHO IS OUR ONLIE HEAD. ANNO 1633'.[165]

Table 1 Tax data for Wigtown and neighbouring burghs (from *Extracts from the Records of the Convention of the Royal Burghs*)

	1535		1597		1612		1649		1670		1690		1705	
	£	%	£	%	£	%	£	%	£	%	£	%	£	%
Ayr	78 15s	2.4	2 3s 4d	2.2	216 13s 4d	2.2	1 8s	1.4	1 14s 8d	1.7	1 14s 8d	1.7	1 1s 4d	1.06
Dumfries	41 5s	1.2	1 16s 8d	1.7	183 6s 8d	1.8	1 13s 4d	1.7	1 13s 4d	1.7	1 18s 4d	1.9	1 18s 4d	1.9
Irvine	45	1.4	1 4s	1.2	120	1.2	1	1	18s	0.9	18s	0.9	10s 6d	0.5
Kirkcudbright	33 15s	1	18s	0.9	90	0.9	16s	0.8	16s	0.8	16s	0.8	6s	0.3
Wigtown	**33 15s**	**1**	**15s**	**0.75**	**75**	**0.75**	**14s**	**0.7**	**14s**	**0.7**	**8s**	**0.4**	**6s**	**0.3**
Whithorn	33 15s	1	5s	0.25	25	0.25	4s	0.2	2s	0.2	2s	0.1	1s	0.05

Although Wigtown was fully involved in the religious and political controversies of the mid-seventeenth century, the burgh and the south-west generally avoided any direct involvement in the civil wars which followed the drawing up of the National Covenant in 1638. The effects on Galloway of the economic recession which struck Scotland in this period, and of the devastating plague epidemic of 1645–48, have not been researched, but it is likely that the region suffered as severely as other parts of the kingdom. Given that a small burgh like Brechin lost perhaps as much as 60% of its population, and most of the larger burghs lost somewhere between 20% and 30%, it is probable that Wigtown's population contracted significantly at this time. Such losses perhaps account for the evident decline in the burgh's fortunes in the second half of the century, demonstrated by the decline in its contribution to the taxes paid via the Convention of Royal Burghs (**table 1**).

The consequences of the disasters of the 1640s may have been offset in part by the economic benefits of Scotland's incorporation into full union with England under the Cromwellian regime but, again, the effects on south-western Scotland have not yet been researched in detail. Wigtown, however, appears to have been one community that was enthusiastically in favour of the union, perhaps because it saw an opportunity to revive its flagging economic fortunes.[166] In 1656, in a report on the trade and customs revenue of Scotland, it was noted that 'there comes sometimes a small boate from England, with salt or coales',[167] but there was otherwise little sign of any significant maritime trade.

Following the return of Charles II from exile, the union with England was dismantled and the king swept away all the changes in government and trade regulations which had been introduced by the Cromwellian regime. Although the burgh had its privileges as a royal burgh restored and reinforced, these changes did not usher in a new golden age. In fact, the period 1660–89 witnessed a return to the religious and political conflicts of before 1638, when the king imposed a new episcopal hierarchy on the Scottish church.

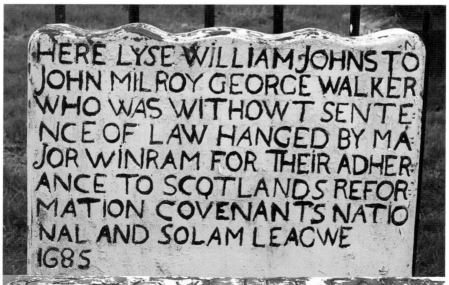

HERE LYSE WILLIAM JOHNSTO
JOHN MILROY GEORGE WALKER
WHO WAS WITHOWT SENTE
NCE OF LAW HANGED BY MA
JOR WINRAM FOR THEIR ADHER
ANCE TO SCOTLANDS REFOR
MATION COVENANTS NATIO
NAL AND SOLAM LEAGWE
1685

FIGURE 11
(top left) The Covenanters'
Monument, Windy Hill
(Richard Oram)
FIGURE 12
(top right) The smaller and
simpler monument down
on the salt marsh, marking
the traditional site where the
two women were drowned
by the rising tide
(Colin Martin)

FIGURE 13
One of the apparently
early eighteenth-century
gravestones commemorating
the 'Wigtown Martyrs'
(Colin Martin)

This time, Galloway became one of the main centres of resistance to the new religious settlement and experienced a period of rigorous policing and, at times, ruthless persecution of those who would not conform. The leading figure was John Graham of Claverhouse, who was active in Galloway from 1678 suppressing conventicles, the illegal gatherings of those who would not accept the episcopalian form of worship. Many of his supposed excesses, however, were more probably the work of his associate, the Dumfriesshire laird Sir Robert Grierson of Lag.[168] In January 1682, Claverhouse was appointed sheriff of Wigtown, replacing Sir Andrew Agnew of Lochnaw, who had refused to take the Test – the oath required of those who held public office that they accepted the royal supremacy. As a result of this prominent role, Claverhouse has often been associated with one of the more grisly episodes in the repression, the possible execution by drowning of two women on the tidal flats to the east of the burgh,[169] though he can be exonerated from any personal involvement. What actually happened at Wigtown is utterly obscure for, despite the major monument to the martyrs erected on Windy Hill in 1858, the smaller monument on the foreshore (**figs 11 & 12**), and the apparently early eighteenth-century gravestones commemorating the two female and three male victims, all said to have been executed in 1685 (**fig 13**),[170] there is no independent or contemporary documentary record of any judicial proceedings or, indeed, of the executions. Controversy has raged since the mid-nineteenth century over whether the martyrdoms did or did not happen, and the issue remains unresolved.

Seventeenth-century trade

In the general round of confirmations and restoration of rights and privileges following the dismantling of the Commonwealth Union under the Cromwellian Protectorate, the council secured a general confirmation of its royal burgh status and all rights and privileges bestowed on it by previous kings by charter of Charles II, issued at Whitehall on 25 May 1662.[171] Among other matters, this charter set out the tolls and charges to be levied by the burgh on burgesses and non-burgesses for the rights to trade in the market, 6s 8d for each free stallage and 13s 4d for each brewer for visiting or inspecting their vessels and measures and restoring them to the just measure yearly; the custom of 2s for each ox or cow, etc, bought within, exported from, or sold in its market, with the custom of 12d for all outside cattle brought into the burgh. Annual and weekly fairs and markets were also confirmed, namely 'the Palme fair and Mid-summer fair, Lambas and Martinmas fairs, and other two horse fairs on the Friday before Midsummer and the Thursday before Lambes, and weekly markets every Thursday from 1 May to 25 December for sale of oxen, sheep and wool, etc, and also weekly markets on Monday for the sale of victual, etc'.

Twenty years later, the government required royal burghs to provide a statement of their setts (constitutions). The return from Wigtown reveals both the smallness of the trading community within Wigtown and the effective running of the burgh by a self-perpetuating oligarchy drawn from among its burgess elite. The council consisted of a provost, two bailies and fifteen councillors, two of whom also served as treasurer and procurator-fiscal. There were no deacons of trades, as 'ther is no Distinctione betwixt merchants and tradesmen'.[172] The council was 'elected' annually, but the old councillors chose the new.[173]

A wider record of the crafts and trades practised in the burgh emerges in the later seventeenth century, pointing to the nature of the broader regional economy. Cloth-manufacture continued to be one of the mainstays of local trade, with 'broadcloth' being produced both within the burgh and in the surrounding country. In the 1680s there were a shoemaker and a tailor.[174] The later seventeenth-century records give no indication that the burgh's merchants were active in international trade as their late medieval counterparts had been. Much of the seaborne trade appears to have been coastal. Council minutes of 1686 and 1687 refer to merchants and ships of Irvine and Lochhead of Kintyre (Campbelltown) with cargoes chiefly of provisions.[175]

There are hints that the main threat by the early seventeenth century was no longer Whithorn but the developing unfree port of Stranraer. In 1613 the burgh secured the support of the Convention of Royal Burghs for a request before the Privy Council for the right to levy an annual impost of 20s on all merchant vessels coming into Loch Ryan, with the exception of ships belonging to other royal burghs.[176] The funds raised, it was claimed, would be used for repairs to Wigtown's harbour, which 'is now become altogidder ruinous'. While Wigtown wished to have the right to levy the toll for a period of thirteen years, the Privy Council was prepared to permit only a five-year licence. Regardless of the actual condition of the harbour at Wigtown, this action appears to have been designed to draw profit away from an emerging rival.

The suggestion of problems with the burgh's finances appears to be confirmed by evidence for a wider economic decline. In 1610, for example, the king granted three vacant burgages on the north side of the town, one immediately to the west of the kirkyard (suggesting that in the early seventeenth century the eastern limit of the burgh was formed by the lane which still divides the cemetery from the last property on Bank Street), to Robert M'Kie, a Wigtown burgess.[177] The population of the burgh, it would seem, was shrinking by this time. While this may have been a consequence of the various outbreaks of epidemic disease which swept through Scotland in the later sixteenth and early seventeenth centuries, there is little evidence for the scale of their impact in the far south-west. Economic recession rather than epidemics alone seems to have been the primary agent for contraction.[178] While the important regional families may have been vying for control of the burgh at this time, Wigtown's actual regional importance appears to have begun to contract.

By the 1680s, the weekly market was said not to have been very busy, although the town still had four 'considerable' annual fairs, held on the fifth Monday in Lent (lasting two days), on 17 June (mainly dealing in horses and cloth), the Lammas fair six weeks later, which also handled cloth, as there was more available later in the season, and the first Monday in November (also two days).[179] The summer horse-fair was attended by borderers from

Annandale, while merchants from Edinburgh, Glasgow and Ayr came to buy woollen cloth.[180] In November and December weekly markets were held selling 'fat kine', frequented by butchers from Dumfries and elsewhere. After four or five such markets 'all the fattest and best kine are sold and gon'.[181] It appears that the cattle trade was of great importance to the burgh and the Machars more generally, and was to be one sector of the economy which performed strongly in the closing decades of the seventeenth and early decades of the eighteenth century. Documentary evidence for the trade is slight before the 1590s, but the large size of the market place suggests that it may in part have been intended to manage stock.[182]

The new royal charter of 1662 had added the right to levy dues on all sheep, cattle and wool crossing the River Cree.[183] Perhaps this indicates the growth of cattle-droving after 1603, and the burgh's determination to monopolise the new trade, or perhaps it was to counter attempts to circumvent the burgh and export goods from another port or by alternative routes. Certainly, a dispute with Dumfries over the arrest of cattle at the crossing of the Cree at Minnigaff in 1598 seems to have been triggered by Wigtown's fear that its market was being circumvented, although the beasts had been bought on behalf of the town of Dumfries which was facing famine due to the collapse of its local market on account of a plague epidemic.[184] Cattle were driven east towards Dumfries and on to Carlisle, probably taking the route across the tidal ford to Creetown until the building of the bridge across the Cree at Newton Stewart. The volume of this traffic is perhaps indicated by the early and large-scale investment by south Wigtownshire lairds in the enclosure of parts of their property as parks for the fattening of stock.[185] Wigtown's place as the principal local cattle market probably saw the first development of the South Field as a park for grazing and watering stock brought in for sale towards the close of the seventeenth century. Daniel Defoe reported in the late seventeenth century that 'The people of Galloway … do not fish, build ships, trade abroad etc, yet they have other business, that is to say, they are meer cultivaters of the earth, and in particular breeders of cattle, such as sheep … and black cattle, of which they send to England'.[186] This repeated emphasis on the predominance of the cattle trade underlines for the first time what was to become one of the principal weaknesses of the regional economy: its over-dependence on one key sector and consequent susceptibility to shifts in the patterns of supply and demand for beef-cattle.

The council records reveal continuing concern over encroachment upon the trading privileges of the burgh, despite the 1662 confirmation charter. Part of the problem appears to have arisen from a failure on the part of the council itself to adhere to the prescribed schedule of markets. In 1683, for example, the council considered that 'the great skaith and damiging of our marckat day' arose from 'not keiping of ane consisting day', especially for the sale of victual, and ordained that no victuals were to be sold other than on

Mondays as the charter stated. There were also mounting concerns over the trade in cloth, with some burgesses apparently attempting to avoid tolls and customs due on broadcloth, or seeking to drive up prices artificially through forestalling. In November 1689, for example, Archibald Fullerton of Cotland was cited to appear before the council on charges of regrating, that is, buying up cloth in the burgh's hinterland and then reselling it at an inflated price in the burgh market.[187] Despite these efforts, the trade in woollen cloth declined during the second half of the century,[188] perhaps indicating that forestalling and regrating were not the only issues affecting Wigtown's trade. In 1688, the poor condition of Bishop Bridge on the road north towards Minnigaff was identified as contributing to the burgh's 'great Lose'. It was therefore agreed that the bridge was to be repaired at the burgh's expense, with two wrights employed to select timbers in the Wood of Cree (in Minnigaff parish, on the east bank of the river upstream from modern Newton Stewart), arrange for their carrying to the site, and then undertake the repairs.[189]

Physical decline?

Maintenance of property within the burgh appears as an issue in council business in the later seventeenth century and may be related to declining prosperity. There was evidently a lack of resources for expenditure on the burgh's public buildings, as well as an apparent reluctance or inability of the burgesses to spend money on their own properties. Even the security of the prison was under question. In November 1681 one William Seton, described as 'lait servitor' to Sir William Maxwell of Monreith, was brought before the burgh court on charges of 'the braiking of this tolbuith for liberating John Gordoune of Grainge'.[190] Seton was accused of using a plough coulter to force the staple from the door-lock, then having entered the tolbooth using it to prise a deal from the floor of one of the chambers to allow Gordon to escape from the chamber below. The main issue here seems to have been absence of provision for the guarding of prisoners and the inadequate structural security of the prison cells in the tolbooth. Considerable expenditure may have followed this event, for in 1684 it was reported that 'The Tolbooth, standing neer the middle of the town, is lately beautify'd with a Pyramis, erected upon a square platforme, upon the top of the steeple, set round with pylasters, which adds a fine ornament to the town'.[191]

In the private sphere, it was the condition of the dykes separating the backlands of properties that was concerning the council. In May and October 1684, the bailies were instructed by the council to inspect kailyard dykes and fine those individuals 'that hes their yeard dycks doune'.[192] In 1685, it was the state of stables in the burgh which they sought to remedy.[193] Poor maintenance of wells appears to have caused problems of water-supply in parts of the burgh, as an ordinance of August 1686 reveals.[194] The tenants of the burgh, both inside and outside the West Port, were to pay 4s towards repair costs, while the tenants outside it, who benefited most from the wells, were to assist the masons and provide them with materials. In 1699 the burgh provided masons and materials for work on the market cross, tolbooth stairs and wells.[195] Shells for the mortar were apparently secured on the east side of the Cree, while peats were to be provided by the burgh tenants for burning the shells for lime.

The cost of this work added significantly to the burgh's financial woes and in 1692, while Wigtown's common good was valued at £693, its debts stood at £2051. Perhaps related to all the costs the town was incurring amidst mounting debts was the fact that it had disposed of most of its assets cheaply, including the majority of the burgh lands, to its overshadowing patrons, the Stewarts of Garlies.[196] In 1692 a government survey of the conditon of Scottish burghs reported that 'In any occasion they have of trade they make use of ther own foot of ther water for ther harbour', but added that 'They have no forraigne trade, and that ther inland trade is verie inconsiderable, and all they have is a retaill of goodes which they bring from Glasgow, Air and Dumfries, the value whereof will amount to 100 lib sterling yearly or thereby, and that they have not vented to ther knowledge above fyve tunn of French wyne these fyve yeares bygone, and that they vent about a hogshead of seck, and a butt of brandie yearly'.[197]

One major problem identified was that the burgh possessed no vessels of its own, pointing to the collapse in its regional trading position in the course of the seventeenth century. The report recognised the vicious circle faced by the burgesses: 'they are neither ship, bark, or boat belonging to them as having no outland trade or convenient pairt', nor were their merchants part-owners of boats based elsewhere. Without involvement in overseas trade there was no incentive for part or full ownership of vessels, with the consequence that there was no incentive to develop the harbour, leading in turn to the effective exclusion of the burgh from overseas trade as its port could not cope with the larger vessels that were beginning to be used. The report also pointed to a stagnant property market, again an indication of the poor economic condition of the burgh. Most houses were owner-occupied rather than let to tenants, and 'the most pairt of the rest are either waist or ruinous, and they have no stranger inhabitantes'.[198]

There was, it seems, little demand for property even in the heart of the burgh where Andrew Symson had mentioned in the previous decade the existence of 'pretty good houses three stories high toward the street, especially on the north side', which was a storey higher than in the average provincial town at that date.[199] Local lairds, like the Dunbars of Baldoon, still had town houses in Wigtown, theirs being on the favoured north side of the main street. It was 'a large, substantial place', which was eventually converted into an inn, the Red Lion, and survived into the mid-twentieth

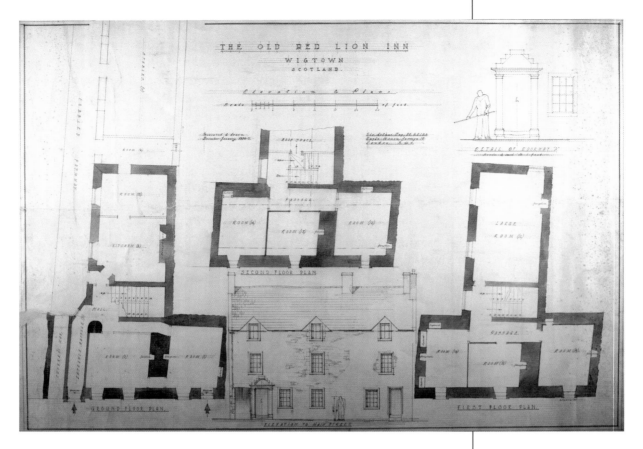

THE OLD RED LION INN
WIGTOWN
SCOTLAND.

century (**fig 14**).[200] As the seat of the sheriff and ecclesiastical courts and the location of the shire's principal market, there was still a need for the leading local landowners to have a residence in the burgh, but there is little evidence that they otherwise conducted much business there.

Running contrary to the picture of general economic decline are indications of efforts to expand provision of certain services to meet local demand. Prominent among these services was teaching. A number of schools, or at least teachers providing a level of private education, existed in the burgh before the 1680s, and Wigtown possessed the only grammar school in the shire.[201] It was small, however, doubling as the parish school, and occupied the ground floor of the tolbooth.[202] In 1682 the council established the position of schoolmaster on a salary of £80 Scots and 10 merks 'chambermaill' (room rent), to 'Dilligentlie and trewlie to teach, learne and instruct the youth both Inglish and Grammer'.[203] Fees were to be 6s 8d for 'ilk bairne within burgh and borrow land' and double for 'ilk Landwart bairne'. To ensure that there was no competition that might undercut the fees charged, the council prohibited other schools from operating within the burgh, with the exception of sewing schools for girls.

FIGURE 14
Architectural plans, elevation and detail of the now demolished Old Red Lion Inn, North Main Street, 1936–37, formerly the town house of the Dunbars of Baldoon (National Archives of Scotland, RHP 30086)

Resource management in an age of crisis

In common with other Scottish provincial towns, Wigtown was at pains in the later seventeenth century to preserve its rights to exploit local resources, particularly of timber and peat. Unlike some northern Scottish burghs,[204] shortage of fuel does not appear to have been an issue at Wigtown, where the extensive mosses on the west side of the Cree provided an apparently inexhaustible source of peat. Coal was being imported by at least 1656 and continued to be brought in through the remainder of the seventeenth century.[205] Physical access to the peat, however, does appear to have been a problem. A council minute of May 1684 reported measures taken to repair the 'throughgait' between the Borrowmoss Bridge and the moss.[206] This involved making a stable track across the moss, composed of heather taken from the muir of Balmeg (Torhousemuir) or Auchleand, and shells.

The moss itself, however, was, like other areas of unimproved ground around the country, starting to experience encroachment for agricultural purposes in the closing decades of the century. At Borrowmoss, tenants on the Earl of Galloway's property were reported in 1687 to have removed the dykes around their arable land and extended cultivation into 'the turf ground', digging up in the process the highway between the burgh and the Bishop Bridge.[207] This encroachment, the earl claimed, had been forced on his tenants by losses of land to the sea, a claim which if true points to significant marine transgression on the west side of the Cree estuary. Such inroads may have had a direct impact on the burgh's harbour, and the reliability of the tidal ford. This inundation of low-lying coastal arable may be related to tidal surges or more regular storm-driven flooding associated with the episode of climatic deterioration loosely labelled as the 'Seven Ill Years', which centred on the 1690s but spanned most of the last two decades of the seventeenth century. Further indication of instability around the estuary occurred in June 1699 when the council was bringing shells for making lime for repairs in the burgh from the eastern shore. It was commented that the ford was 'to be doubted' and, if it were impassable, Lord Galloway's boat be sought to transport the materials.[208]

There is other evidence in the council minutes of pressure on resources during the 1690s, when climatic variations in the 'little ice age' produced weather-events that affected crop-growing conditions. The issue of straying 'nolt or naigs' eating grass on other men's property appears to have been a constant irritant and source of disputes. An isolated ordinance of 1694 concerning the cutting of grass on the baulks between the rigs of cultivated ground, or from meadows, which belonged to other men, points, perhaps, to shortages of fodder.[209] A related but more general issue concerned individuals who kept cattle or horses but who lacked private land or a right to any share in the burgh's common grazings upon which to pasture them. This was a significant enough problem in 1687 for the council to ordain against those who lacked pasture but were grazing animals instead on what they claimed were 'Waist Aikers' or in the common vennels, causing obstruction and nuisance.[210]

The long eighteenth century

The end of the seventeenth century and the beginning of the eighteenth was a period of regular crop-failures, crises in food-supply and localised famine across Scotland. Peat and firewood were increasingly difficult to obtain, as was timber for building.[211] The general view is that this situation began to improve only in the second half of the eighteenth century. Despite its relative isolation from the expanding economic heartland of Scotland, Galloway, by the late eighteenth century, 'was in the vanguard of agrarian development' but several of its principal landowners had been leading figures in agricultural experimentation in the earlier part of the century.[212]

It has been claimed that agricultural change in Wigtownshire was started late and suddenly when the earls of Galloway bought the estate of Baldoon, and rouped (auctioned) the new leases.[213] Their investment and experimentation, however, was occurring at a time when capital was supposedly scarce, the regional economy stagnant, and the spirit of entrepreneurialism suppressed. Mixed agriculture, however, was less susceptible to market fluctuations, and most good land in Galloway was not far from the coast, from which produce could be shipped to neighbouring areas which were more industrial, especially England.[214] The advantages of geography were well recognised in the early nineteenth-century agricultural reports which promoted the further development of Improvement practices: 'The richest lands lie upon the coast; where the means of improvement are to be met with in the greatest abundance'.[215] Most of the produce was exported by sea to England, though cattle were usually driven overland, mainly to markets in Norfolk and Suffolk.[216]

There may have been hopes for a revival in the local economy during the discussion of parliamentary union between Scotland and England. The burgh's political life was then dominated by the 5th Earl of Galloway, who was a member of the so-called Court Party in the Scottish Parliament and inclined towards the benefits of union. In 1703 the earl arranged for the election of his recently widowed brother-in-law, John Clerk of Penicuik, as MP for the burgh, while Galloway's kinsman, the 2nd Duke of Queensberry, engineered Clerk's rapid rise in the political establishment in Edinburgh. Clerk became one of the Commissioners treating for the union with England, and his detailed knowledge of Scotland's financial state and the condition of the economy was to be a major factor in his role in promoting the Union Bill in the Scottish Parliament.[217] The Earl of Galloway – and Wigtown –

may have hoped for some economic betterment from union, but the burgh's fortunes showed no significant revival after the Act of Union of 1707. This had opened up trade between Scotland and England and gave Scottish merchants legal access to the English colonies with which they had already been dealing illicitly for decades. Unfortunately, it was the better-established trading burghs on the west coast, such as Ayr, which benefited most from the developing Atlantic trade.

The continuing generally poor state of the Scottish economy after the Union was one contributory factor in the upsurge of support for the exiled Stuarts in the early eighteenth century. Such sympathies in Galloway, however, were confined mainly to some of the leading families in northern and eastern areas, headed by the Gordons of Lochinvar, Viscounts Kenmure. The 6th Viscount was a leading figure in the 1715 Jacobite rebellion, raising a small local force and marching into north-west England to join the Earl of Derwentwater. He was defeated, however, and captured by government soldiers at Preston – the main action in the rising bypassed Galloway. Indifference or hostility towards the Jacobite cause may have been largely a consequence of the entrenched support within Galloway for Presbyterianism and strong hostility to the Episcopalianism and Roman Catholicism with which the exiled Stuarts were associated.

The forfeiture and execution of the 6th Viscount Kenmure broke the power of the Jacobite Gordons and removed any pro-Stuart leadership from the region. Whig and Hanoverian support in Galloway appears to have been almost universal after 1715 and there was no real local sympathy for subsequent Jacobite action. The '45 rising appears to have had no impact at all in terms of support for the rebellion, but the political and legal reforms that were introduced in the wake of its suppression had important ramifications for local proprietors. One of the most profound consequences was the abolition of heritable jurisdictions in 1747. This, at a stroke, removed the private jurisdictional franchises exercised through barony and regality courts, as well as the heritable tenure of legal offices, such as sheriffships. At Wigtown the effect was to end the long hereditary tenure of the sheriffship by the Agnews of Lochnaw, whose local influence contracted to the area around their estates in the west of the shire. In reality, however, real influence locally had lain with the Stewart earls of Galloway since the sixteenth century and their interest continued to dominate Wigtown's politics into the later nineteenth century.

The agricultural improvement programme which some of the early eighteenth-century lairds saw as the key to economic revival was not universally popular. Enclosure, as practised on the Earl of Galloway's property, stoked bitter resentment among the small tenants who were being squeezed out to make room for larger, consolidated landholdings. Hostility erupted in 1723–24 in the so-called Levellers' rising, protesting at the building of stone dykes to divide up the land. The impact of this resistance appears to have been very variable and localised. While it may have slowed the move towards agricultural improvement in some parts of Galloway, in the Machars enclosure continued. Indeed, the town council of Wigtown decreed in 1725 that part of the burgh lands should be 'sett out in parcels and inclosed'. Four years later they let the burgh moss, though the poor were allowed to take peat in return for labour 'for to help to drain the said moss'.[218] As improved farming methods were introduced more widely, the numbers needed to work the land were reduced. There were no rapidly growing towns in the area to absorb these people, so the eighteenth century saw much emigration. Sources towards the end of the century expressed the hope that the spirit of improvement would soon reach Galloway.

In Wigtown parish by the 1790s 'The face of the country is improving daily, not only by the cultivation bestowed upon the land, but by a passion for planting which shows itself among the landholders'. Farm houses had 'improved very much within the last twenty years. They are often covered with slate, and divided into convenient apartments. Sheds and straw-yards are coming into general use'.[219] Enthusiasm for reclamation of coastal flats was running high and the extensive tidal areas to the east of the burgh were seen as ripe for embankment and conversion to arable land: 'Wigton Bay, for many thousand acres, has a rich clay bottom; and the practicability of laying it dry is confidently talked of by people of knowledge in embanking, and has long been a favourite idea of the Earl of Selkirk'.[220] 'It is not above 20 years since enclosing became general, during which time it has been carried on with spirit … Even the borough-acres, which, till of late, were all of them open … are now almost wholly enclosed'. Land near the coast was improved with shell marl from across the Cree, while inland farms used lime imported from England.[221] Most of the reporters to the *Statistical Account* were enthusiasts for Improvement, but it is evident that the developments which they lauded had not been achieved without a human price and opposition.

As early as the 1720s, some forward-looking lairds had recognised the advantages of concentrating their efforts on cattle-breeding for the meat trade, but the result by the end of the century was a possible over-dependence on agricultural production. Despite some efforts to develop industry in Galloway, the region remained overwhelmingly agricultural and exposed to all the hazards of such an economic and social basis. One commentator observed that by 1810

> The chief, and indeed almost the only exports from Galloway consist of grain, wool, sheep and black cattle, which are sent … to England, and to some other parts of Scotland. The imports are lime, coals, wool, all sorts of groceries and manufactured goods, chiefly from England. Wood is sometimes imported directly from America, and both wood and

iron from the Baltic. But though attempts have been made to enlarge the commerce of the country by trading to the West Indies, as well as to America and the Baltic on a larger scale; and also to embark in the herring fishery – these attempts have never hitherto been successful.[222]

'A part of that [the crop] for sale, especially of the oats, is made into meal, and sold in the market of Wigton; but the bulk of it is exported to Whitehaven or Liverpool, to Ayr, Irvine, or Greenock.' Some potatoes were grown, and one farmer grew turnips, which had 'proved remarkably good', and were used to feed young cattle over the winter. Almost all the pasture was for cattle, with few sheep kept.[223]

Galloway, like much of rural Scotland, participated in the early phases of the Industrial Revolution, but lost out when steam power led to the concentration of resources in the large conurbations with plenty of labour and good transport networks. The woollen industry was 'probably the first manufacturing industry to be revitalised by capital investment'. Several water-powered mills were built elsewhere in Galloway after the 1770s, mostly by local entrepreneurs or merchants, but these were involved principally in the processing of imported cotton rather than local wool or flax. 'The linen industry was never of any great importance in Galloway … The cotton industry was of more lasting importance.'[224] The late 1780s saw 'cotton-spinning mania', with major mills leading to the growth or even creation of new villages at Newton Douglas, Castle Douglas, and Gatehouse of Fleet. The boom, however, was short-lived, ending with the disruption of international trade which followed the outbreak of the Napoleonic Wars. One contemporary commentator observed that 'Previous to the commencement of the present war, near 600 hands might be employed in the different manufactures, of which the cotton spinning at Gate-House was by far the most extensive. Since that period, the number has daily been on the decline'.[225] The cotton mills at Gatehouse and Newton Stewart failed despite good water-power and good roads offering access to markets.[226]

In 1793 it was noted that

In the town of Wigton, as in almost all the other towns of Galloway, there has long been a want of industry. Something of a manufacturing spirit, however, having lately arisen in this part of the country, two small manufactures, the one of wool and the other of cotton, were introduced into this town, about a year and a half ago. In the former of these, which employs between 30 and 40 persons, the wool is manufactured into plaiding and flannel, especially the former, and sent mostly to the English market. The latter, which would have employed about 20 persons, was soon hurt after its commencement, and is now almost entirely ruined, by the iniquity of the times.[227]

A small 'wool manufactory' on the River Bladnoch at Waulkmill had, by 1792, 40 workers making 'plaiding and flannel' for export to England.[228] There was a tannery down below the church.[229]

Access to capital for investment appears to have been difficult and may have been a major factor in limiting local entrepreneurs. Something of a vicious circle, however, may have resulted, for the absence of economic growth in the area occasioned by a lack of investment may have deterred would-be investors from speculating in the region. One key manifestation of this may be seen in the underprovision of banking in south-western Scotland. There had been some early moves, marked by the establishment in 1769 of the Ayr Bank (Douglas, Heron & Co), with a branch in Dumfries. Its collapse in 1772 may have had long-term consequences, for it was said to have 'dampened spirits' and inhibited agricultural improvements.[230] The first bank in Galloway was the Bank of Scotland, which opened a branch in Wigtown in 1784, followed by one in Kirkcudbright in 1789–90. A branch of the British Linen Bank was opened in Wigtown in 1785, but after the death of its agent in 1801 it was moved to Newton Stewart.[231] The Galloway Banking Company was established in Castle Douglas in 1806, and by 1810 had branches in Dumfries and Kirkcudbright.[232] Apart from these, the nearest banks were in Dumfries, which had a branch of the British Linen Company from 1771, and the Bank of Scotland from 1774.[233] The Galloway Banking Company was established in 1806, based in Castle Douglas, and survived until 1821. In 1810 it had branches in Dumfries and Kirkcudbright.[234]

Some insight into the prosperity of the burgh is afforded by the more systematic tax records which survive from the later eighteenth century. The Shop Tax in 1787–88, for example, was paid by James McColm, innkeeper/vintner (£5 value), and William McConnell Esq, agent for the Bank of Scotland (£6). The following year they were joined by a Lieutenant Dunn (£8), whose trade is not given. None of these, revealingly, is described as a merchant.[235] The limited number of prosperous traders in the burgh is perhaps a reflection of its continuing decline in regional significance. By the 1790s Stranraer, with 1602 inhabitants, was the 61st largest community in Scotland, while Newton Stewart, with 1100 inhabitants, was in 97th place, and Wigtown, with 1032 inhabitants, 105th.[236] Wigtown had lost its status as the largest burgh of the shire to its western rival, which was flourishing on the back of the burgeoning Irish traffic, and had also been overtaken by the new planned community of Newton Stewart which had been established at the western end of the bridge over the Cree. The emergence of the route between Newton Stewart and Stranraer as the principal east–west artery through the shire served to reinforce their status as the most important centres for trade and travellers: Wigtown was by-passed and struggling.

Even its importance as the main centre in the Machars was under threat. The other growing ports in the area were Garlieston, Isle of Whithorn and

Portpatrick.[237] The recent foundation of Garlieston was clearly regarded as a success, but it may have been drawing inhabitants from already established centres in Galloway rather than attracting colonists from further afield. The threat from Garlieston was complicated by the influence of the Stewarts of Galloway in Wigtownshire politics. During the eighteenth century the parliamentary votes for Whithorn and Wigtown were controlled by the earls of Galloway.

Poor landward communications may have been a further significant bar to economic development. The regional road system as late as the 1700s appears to have followed the lines established in the Middle Ages and depended on ferries or old, narrow bridges. The Bridge of Cree was built in 1703, and in 1728 the first stone bridge over the Bladnoch was constructed.[238] The eighteenth century saw radical change with the construction of military roads. Ian Donnachie observed that 'Galloway shared with the Highlands an impenetrability which alarmed the military mind of the Hanoverians. The fact that this wild and inhospitable countryside had to be traversed to reach Ireland was an additional incentive to the strategists to press forward the improvement of communications between England and Ireland'.[239] Built 'to open a speedy, and certain communication between Great Britain and Ireland; especially with regard to the passage of the Troops from one Kingdom to the other, whenever the Exigency of Affairs may require it',[240] the military road ran 'from Bridge of Sark, near Gretna Green, to Port Patrick, with a northern arm from Stranraer to Ballantrae'.[241] There was already some sort of road along this route in the Middle Ages, but it underwent a major reconstruction, mainly between 1763 and 1765 by Major Rickson, under the overall supervision of Major Caulfield.[242]

The provision of this major east–west artery, reinforced in 1796 when the area's first Turnpike Act led to the construction of a road from Dumfries to Castle Douglas, saw the further marginalising of the communities which lay at a distance from the new roads. The Machars derived little benefit from a road which directed traffic towards rival ports in west Wigtownshire, and this situation became entrenched in the following 20 to 30 years which saw the construction of other new roads, including Newton Stewart to Portpatrick, which formed the basis for the modern road network.[243] Government investment in the new roads led to similar development of harbour facilities at Portpatrick and Stranraer. Wigtown, however, did not miss out entirely on this investment in communications, as 'The roads are getting fast into a state of repair, and are let to be kept so for 10 years. The bridges in the parish are upheld from the county funds, and are in excellent condition'.[244] This positive gloss, however, could not disguise the fact that, since the construction of the bridge at Newton Stewart in 1703 and the decline of the Creetown ford, Wigtown lay on a loop road that required a major detour from the principal route through Galloway.

Recent research has emphasised that 'The development of many small ports was associated with very real, local economic needs to an extent far greater than their share of tonnage or value suggests'.[245] This was especially true during the eighteenth century, with religious and political stability, and agricultural improvement, but before the development of better inland communications. Ports which were successful at this time show a greater increase in population than the regional average, Stranraer being the most obvious success in Galloway. The eighteenth century also saw a new customs organisation, with head ports at Stranraer, Wigtown and Dumfries, which, *prima facie*, suggests that Wigtown was still a leading regional trading centre. The new structure placed the burgh in control of 35 miles (56km) of coastline, from Luce Bay to Carsluith. Although the eighteenth century saw some growth in coastal shipping, Wigtown's position as the head port was mainly administrative, and Garlieston became much more successful as an active conduit for trade than both Wigtown and the Isle of Whithorn.[246]

Documents from the first decade of the eighteenth century give us a vivid glimpse of Wigtown's maritime trade, and its harbour, and reveal a degree of recovery from the dire conditions reported in 1692.[247] A company consisting of the Earl of Galloway, James Dunbar of Mochrum, William Coltrane/Coutram of Drummond, Patrick his son, who was provost of Wigtown, bailie John McKie, bailie Simon Gullane, and William Russell, bought the ship *Katherine* at Ayr, making the final payment in 1701. A ketch from Glasgow bought timber and tar to repair her. They employed a skipper and eight seamen, one of them described as the carpenter. They or their agents travelled all over Galloway buying animal skins for processing for export. This involved digging holes for processing the skins, and carrying the skins to and from this working area, described as 'the hoolls'.[248]

In 1700 the company had goods from Holland in its storehouse. In 1701 the *Katherine* sailed to Nantes with skins and returned with wine and salt. In 1702 the company imported 321 bolls of French salt, and there was at least one other trip to Holland.[249] The ship also made shorter trips, carrying wool to the Clyde, and dressed leather to Liverpool. The imported goods were carried up the hill to the company's storehouse, or occasionally the laigh tolbooth, and from there sold on to merchants and private customers all over Galloway. A list of those owing the company money in 1701 included ten merchants, four shoemakers, the minister and the town clerk in Wigtown, and five merchants, a dyer and the minister in Whithorn. Others were in Creetown, Glenluce, Kirkcudbright, Minnigaff, New Galloway, and Newton Stewart.

The 'harbour' of Wigtown at this time was really just a quay at the river-mouth, shown in an illustration by William Daniell in 1815 (**fig 15**). There was little space beside it due to the steeply rising ground, so the company's storehouse seems to have been located up the hill. When the ship was due, men went out at low tide to erect poles to mark the navigation channel for

the ship to come in at high tide ('putting up the pearches for bringing in the ship'), and the same when she left. They also had to pay for a pilot. It would not have been a safe place for a ship to sit for long. Sometimes the *Katherine* lay at the Isle of Whithorn, but over the winter she was pulled up from 'the creek' to a 'boatyard', where there was a large hollow which served as a simple dry dock. When she was inside it a wall was built on the seaward side to protect her from storms. Here she was repaired using local wood. When it was time to prepare for the next voyage, the wall was cast down and she was pulled down to the harbour again, where she was loaded with stones for ballast and whins for dunnage.[250]

Around 1712 there were three ships listed as belonging to Wigtown, with a total tonnage of 104 (average 35), the only vessels within the customs precinct. By 1759 the tonnage for the precinct had increased to 181.[251] In 1760, however, Pococke described ships docking at Isle of Whithorn, 'They export barley, and import plank and iron from Gottenburgh in Sweden, and send it by boats to Wigtown, as the entrance and harbour there are not good'.[252] Meal and other farm products were exported north to the Clyde and south as far as Preston. Imports included lime and coal, manufactured goods, and shell and lime from across the bay. Smaller vessels were involved in fishing, although most of that activity may have been based on fixed stake nets in the estuary, from which fish were removed at low tide. 'There is a small salmon fishing in the river of Bladenoch ... The inhabitants of Wigton have the privilege of fishing salmon in a particular part of the water of Cree, opposite to the town itself ... Various kinds of white fish, especially flounders, are taken in the bay of Wigton'.[253] In 1793 there were sixteen part-time fishermen.[254] Again, however, the vagaries of the shifting sand- and mud-banks in Wigtown Bay and the better access to deep waters enjoyed by ports further south and west meant that the burgh never developed a significant role as a fishing port.

Smuggling was a major problem (or industry) in the later eighteenth century, particularly of tea and brandy from the Isle of Man. The effect was that 'the fair trader is quite discouraged ... the morals of numbers of people debauched, and our country drained of its coin', which instead of financing local manufactures was 'carried over to the Isle of Man, whence it's directly transferred to France, to strengthen the hands of our declared enemies'. In 1778 the government offered an amnesty to smugglers if they joined the army or navy, and the excise-officer in Wigtown remembered about 500 men in the area doing so.[255] Troops were brought in in an attempt to crack down on smuggling, and in Wigtown were accommodated in a house known for long after as 'the Barracks', 'on the right side of the street known as Botany'.[256]

From the mid-eighteenth century it is possible to trace efforts to revive the burgh's fortunes and to restore its place as the social, if not the commercial, heart of the shire. Expenditure on building projects is one indicator. Private houses were, it seems, not part of this process by 1760, when Wigtown was described as consisting 'of one broad street which, about the cross and market house, is like a square, and the houses are tolerable, but below it is narrower, with thatched houses on each side'. Usually one of the first public structures to be rebuilt as a reflection of prosperity, growing population, and the good taste of the burgh elite, was the parish church, but not in Wigtown. The same visitor in 1760 described the church as old, with its large Gothic east window walled up.[257] The medieval church appears to have survived with minor modifications down to 1730, and c 1770 underwent a programme of reconstruction, and a complete re-ordering of the interior. It was probably at this time that three galleries were added, perhaps reflecting the growing population of the town.[258] In the 1790s there was no manse, just a rent allowance.[259] In addition to the Church of Scotland, a Seceding congregation had established itself in 1745 and an Anti-Burgher meeting-house was built at the west end of the burgh in 1750.[260] This also had galleries added in 1785, so that it could hold 400 people.[261] Despite the size of their new church, in 1793 there were only 191 Seceders plus 27 Cameronians in the town.[262]

Although the parish church did not see significant reconstruction, money was spent on two other symbols of prosperity. The grammar school, which had been housed on the ground floor of the tolbooth, finally got its own building, construction starting in 1712.[263] However, it was described as unused and needing repair in 1717 and 1721.[264] By the 1790s the school was on a sounder footing, and was described as 'a good grammar school', with a master and an assistant, and 60 to 100 scholars, who were taught Latin and Greek. 'All children, even those of the poorest people, are instructed in reading English, in writing, and the common rules of arithmetick'.[265] At one time the school had, unusually, also taught French.[266]

More immediately successful was the replacement of the principal symbol of burghal pride, its Town House. The tolbooth described by Symson was demolished with gunpowder in 1747, and in 1747–49 a new Town House, with a ground-floor arcaded covered market, was built by bailie Samuel Kennan, mason, to a design by John Douglas. By 1774 this was already 'ruinous and decayed', and was again rebuilt, this time with a fashionable tall spire, in 1776. The original design was altered, being heightened to allow a 'handsome ballroom' to be inserted, paid for by the masonic lodge. It also included the parish school-room, indicating that the separate school building repaired in 1721 had finally been abandoned.[267] There was a ground-floor vaulted cell, which can still be seen, incorporated in the later nineteenth-century town hall, and further prison accommodation was provided on the upper floors.[268]

Significant changes to the physical appearance of the core of the burgh began soon after Pococke's 1760 visit. The West Port at the mouth of High Vennel, and the East Port opposite Bank House, were demolished in 1761 because they were too narrow for carriages, and in the case of the West Port divided the upper town from the lower.[269] They had been flanked by houses sticking out at right-angles to the rest, one of which survived into the later nineteenth century (see **map 7**).[270] The High Street, at the head of the town, was so narrow 'that two carts could hardly pass each other'. Towards the end of the eighteenth century the houses were rebuilt further back.[271] A major townscape development was the laying out of the square in 1809.[272] The garden and bowling green replaced 'a broad expanse, covered with rank grass and nettles, in the shelter of which hens and ducks deposited their eggs. This vast space was also the site of the various middens of the burgesses, these being located several yards in front of the houses – little footpaths leading to them from the dwelling-houses being visible through the grass'. There were also peat stacks.[273] The town officers were given new uniforms, and the streets regularly cleaned; the square was furnished with railings and eight lamp posts, and was finished off with a new market cross in 1816.[274]

In 1779 the *Dumfries Weekly Journal* advertised the lease of 'a mansion, newly built … being in a good part of town on the great road from Whithorn and Galloway House to Newton Stewart'. The particulars suggested that it had the potential for use as a coaching inn. Signs of a significant change in the use of the central space in the burgh may also be seen in the fact that two large houses were also advertised for sale on the south side of Main Street, which had previously been the less-favoured side and the location of smaller and lower houses. Expansion seems to have progressed rapidly in the closing years of the century, it being commented in 1793 that 'Upon the whole, the better sort of the inhabitants in town, now generally occupy pretty good houses, and live rather in a genteel style', and in 1797 four fields were advertised for sale as potential development sites for new housing.[275]

The burgh was breaking out of its medieval limits. There were already in the mid-eighteenth century a few houses on the west side of Agnew Crescent, and some cottages south-east of the Town House, at the entrance of the later Harbour Road (**map 5**).[276] The early years of the nineteenth century saw the fuller development of Agnew Crescent and Acre Place, and at least four of the town-centre houses were occupied by retired planters from Jamaica.[277] Significant money was beginning to return to the burgh. Rochdale House, later Applegarth, now at the entrance to Harbour Road, but pre-dating the road, was built by the minister in 1814, replacing an older manse in Low Vennel.[278] Such developments seem to have stimulated the growth of a social scene. The presence in 1746 of a dancing-master suggests the growth of a 'season' with formal gatherings.[279] Another marker of social devlopment was the establishment in 1794 of a subscription library, which soon had 63 members, including seven women.[280] It was members of this developing urban elite who, in 1797, in response to the threat of invasion, established a corps of Volunteers.[281]

The Window Tax records, between 1753 and 1799, though using varying criteria, demonstrate that there were several large houses in Wigtown. At first, from 1753 to 1758, the tax was only levied on houses with ten windows or more. For these years the average number of houses paying the tax was ten; two houses had as many as nineteen windows, while the minister's house had fourteen. From 1758 the threshold was lowered to six windows, bringing the number of taxed houses in Wigtown up to 20. The number fluctuated somewhat, mainly due to houses lying empty. The Agnews of Ochiltree (David, then Nathaniel) had a house with nineteen windows (the later Bank House), as did James Maxwell, innkeeper. Others included the minister and the doctor, both with fourteen. Over the years some people managed to reduce slightly the number of windows on which they paid tax. By the mid-1760s the doctor had gone, and the new minister had only eleven windows. A newcomer to the list by 1769 was Robert Murray, wine merchant, with seventeen windows.[282]

New in 1785 was William McConnell, for the Customs House, with eleven windows. The following year John Brown, Controller of Customs, was paying tax on seventeen windows (this was the back part of the Old Bank House, 7/8 South Main Street).[283] In the 1780s the largest houses were owned by the Controller of Customs, the innkeepers, minister, doctor, writers and merchants, with the Agnew family still owners of one of the largest houses.[284]

The Inhabited House Tax of 1778–98 records the value rather than the size of houses. In 1778 thirteen people paid the tax, including Alexander Burton, merchant, and William Mitchell, innkeeper, with houses valued at £5, and

William McConnell Esq (probably No 7/8 South Main Street) and Nathaniel Agnew, both with houses valued at £6.[285] As these were high on the window tax list, perhaps these were old family town houses, not new, fashionable and more expensive houses. James McColm, another innkeeper, had a house valued at £7, and top of the list was John McCulloch Esq at £8. In the second year Robert Murray, wine merchant, entered the list (£5). By 1787 there were fourteen houses paying, including the customs house (£7), while in 1788 Lieutenant Dunn entered the list (£8). The final list, for 1797–98, included William McConnell and the collector of customs (both £10), two writers (£8), an innkeeper (£7), a surgeon (£6), and two writers, two innkeepers, a merchant and an accountant (all £5).[286]

The sett of the town council remained the same. Mid-eighteenth-century provosts, despite the abolition of heritable jurisdictions, included the Earl of Galloway and his heir, Lord Garlies.[287] It was common at this time for landowners to wish to control towns, for the sake of the town's right to help choose the MP, and for councils to accept a gentry provost for the sake of the business and patronage he could bring to the town.[288]

The increase in the population of the parish between 1755 and 1793 was put down by its minister wholly to the growth of the town, including unemployed agricultural workers moving in, and also 'the influx of people from Ireland … of whom above 100 at present reside within the town'.[289] In common with the attitudes expressed towards these migrants elsewhere in the *Statistical Account*, the minister of Wigtown had a poor opinion of their quality: 'It must, however, be confessed, that many of them [tradesmen and day labourers] are still in an indigent state; as almost all the Irish families which have settled here, are in a condition of abject poverty'.[290] Over 40 regular paupers were supported by the kirk session, but, as the minister expressed it, 'The place is infested by swarms of strolling beggars'.[291]

The most numerous occupations in the parish in 1793 were 62 day labourers, 56 farm servants (30 male and 26 female), 54 female domestic servants, 35 farmers, 25 weavers, 16 fishermen (part-time), 16 carpenters, 16 shopkeepers, 15 tailors, 14 shoemakers, 12 masons and 12 seamen.[292] Those who paid tax on six or more windows in 1798–99 included five merchants, five writers, four innkeepers, an accountant, a surgeon and a vintner. Those paying on fewer than six windows included five carters, four weavers, three labourers, three wrights and two masons.[293]

A post office was opened in 1705, and a regular postal service was operating by 1707.[294] A Friendly Society was founded in 1795. Its stated aims were to provide an allowance to members during sickness, to pay a 'superannuation allowance' to members, and to contribute to funeral costs. Only working men between 18 and 40, with no criminal conviction and no current infirmity, could join. If any disability came to light within the first two years, membership could be withdrawn.[295]

c 1820–1914

Despite the continuing programmes of agricultural improvement, Galloway's regional economy remained significantly poorer than that of central or eastern Scotland through its overwhelming dependence on agricultural production.[296] While there was a growing market for that produce as Britain's urban labouring populations boomed, the poor state of the communications network in southern Wigtownshire perhaps hindered fuller integration into that growing market. The development of steam shipping and more regular services from Galloway harbours to north-western England, however, began to open up wider markets for cattle, and consequently, agriculture became more profitable. Wigtown, however, does not seem to have reaped much of the benefit, remaining principally a small 'gentry' town serving the business needs of a small group of lairds, substantial farmers and professionals. In 1832 it was described as: 'a neat clean small Town' though not apparently growing. 'Its Harbour is about half a mile from the Town, and it does not seem to have much Trade'.[297] By 1839 'little or no business' was being done at Wigtown's fairs, 'and they are now fallen into complete neglect'.[298] There were 'Some small manufactures in Wigtown', and a tannery.[299] This picture of general decline, however, needs to be offset by the contradictory evidence for the prosperity of a segment of its population and, as discussed below, the gradual introduction of a series of fashionable architectural and social symbols. In terms of population, the peak was reached in the 1851 census (**table 2**).

In the early nineteenth century the loop of the River Bladnoch on which

FIGURE 16
The new harbour, now deserted (Paula Martin)

Table 2 Population data

	1755	1790s	change 1755–1790s	1801	1811	1821	1831	1841	1851	change 1841–51	1861	1871	1881	change 1851–81	1891	1901	1911	1921	1931	1941	1951	1961	1971	1981
Whithorn (parish)	1412	1890	34%	1904	1935	2361	2415	2795	3001		2934	2906	2929		2574	2235	2140	1989	1796		1910	1726	1620	1454
Whithorn (burgh)		756					1305	1513	1652	9%	1652	1577	1653	0%	1403	1188	1170	1033	951		1068	990	988	983
Newton Stewart								2171	2599	29%	2535	2873	3070	18%	2738	2598	2063	1831	1914		1997	1981	1883	
Stranraer								4889	5738	17%	6315	5977	6415	12%	6193	6036	6444	6138	6527		8618	9250	9853	
Wigtown (parish)	1032	1350	31%	1475	1711	2042	2337	2562	2824		2637	2306	2198		1911	1747	1716	1607	1531		1608	1403	1288	
Wigtown (burgh)		1032						1972	2232	13%	2124	1847	1792	- 20%	1509	1386	1369	1299	1261		1376	1199	1118	

the old harbour was situated was having increasing problems with silting, and was eventually cut off and a new channel created. The town council therefore was forced into the decision to create a new harbour further up the Bladnoch, to the south-east of the town. Subscriptions were raised in 1817, and the new harbour was opened in 1822 (**fig 16**).[300] This, together with the establishment at the same time of the distillery, led to the creation of the village of Bridgeton or Bladnoch. This soon became the home of other industrial enterprises such as a foundry, a coachmaker and a shipbuilder.[301] The Bladnoch distillery, founded in 1817 by John and Thomas Maclellan at the head of the village and on the river, consisted of 'a square pile of buildings erected round a court-yard'. By 1839 it was employing about 20 labourers and consuming about 16,000 bushels of barley annually.[302] It was enlarged and modernised in 1878, so that it covered two acres and by the 1880s its annual output was 51,000 gallons.[303]

The new harbour could be visited by vessels of up to 300 tons.[304] This major piece of expenditure was directly related to the growth in agricultural produce available for export. Consisting of a riverside quay and a large rectangular basin (now filled in), it attracted a flourishing coastal trade, mainly exporting cattle, sheep, grain and potatoes, and importing coal, lime and manures. 'The town flourished afresh'.[305] In 1832 about fourteen ships belonged to the town, amounting to about 883 tons. There were 76 outward-bound voyages and 90 inward.[306] Towards the end of the period, 'of late years, cheddar cheese to a large extent has been exported', marking the development locally of industrial-scale dairy farming, a new business development that was to remain important in the local economy down to the 1980s.[307] Even with the development of the harbour there was little fishing. Fishing is not listed as an occupation in any of the *Trades Directories*, though there is a gravestone to a fisherman who died in 1909 at the age of 79.[308]

By 1839 the Bank of Scotland had left Wigtown, which suggests that the level of business in the town was inadequate to support a permanent establishment. There was, however, a branch of the British Linen Bank, which had arrived in 1825, appointing John Black, writer, as its agent, and a private bank.[309] The lack of financial services in what was still the chief town of the shire points to the low level of business activity. The arrival of the railway in 1875 marked a decisive change, witnessing the rebuilding of the two bank offices, and the arrival of a third bank.[310] By the 1890s the British Linen, Clydesdale and National Banks all had a presence.[311]

It was not that there were no earlier attempts to boost business potential, particularly by improving communications. In 1825, for example, the first steamer services started, and soon there was a regular fortnightly service to Whitehaven and Liverpool. In 1829 the Wigtown Steam Navigation Company was established, and in 1835 it ordered the first *Countess of Galloway* to be built in Glasgow. It also constructed a large warehouse between Knockacre

Table 3 Shipping in Wigtown customs precinct (data from *Slater's Directories*)

	1831	1850	1869	1876	1898	1902	1909	1913
Locally owned vessels	14	69	48	39	18			
average tonnage	63	57	59	49	39			
British/foreign in	90		571	1029	246	3	4	3
average tonnage			54	39.5	59	477	154	133
British/foreign out	76		344	1052	257			
average tonnage			71	40	58			
Coastal in					233	202	185	168
average tonnage					60	83	67	79
Coastal out					251	160	204	198
average tonnage					59	89	70	81
Locally registered fishing boats					78			
average tonnage					1.5			

and Beechwood.[312] The overall shipping numbers within the customs precinct are shown in **table 3**. The beneficial impact of such connections was well understood, as expressed by one contemporary writer:

> It need hardly be observed that steam navigation has been of essential service to Wigtownshire in general. That mode of communication now exists between her principal ports and Liverpool and Whitehaven, in addition to the intercourse with Glasgow from Stranraer. These open a quick and ready market both for grain and live stock, and for ready money, at the current price; whereas, in former times, sales were scarcely ever met by cash. Travelling corn-dealers bought up the grain (by bills) with a view of shipment to the English market, and being seldom men of capital, and their trade precarious, a greater proportion became bankrupt than in almost any other class. Those who purchased cattle, to drive for sale to England, were much in the same predicament, and likewise payed by means of bills. Hence the Wigtonshire farmers were frequently exposed to risk, and not seldom suffered the severest losses. Steam has changed this, though it has lessened trade with Ireland.[313]

A latecomer to this maritime transport system, which operated between 1894 and 1931, was the Argyll and Wigtown Steam-Ship Company.[314] Wigtown's trade was only for 'local requirements', however, and the advent of steam shipping actually reduced its importance, as vessels from England called at Garlieston rather than Wigtown.[315] The burgh still had the apparatus of an important port: a customs-house, with a precinct covering an area

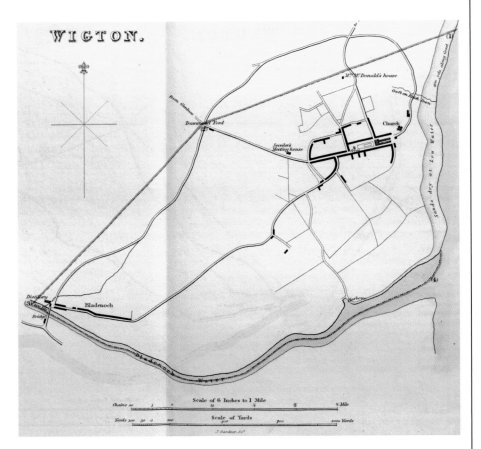

WIGTON.

HISTORIC WIGTOWN:
ARCHAEOLOGY AND
DEVELOPMENT

from the Mull of Galloway to the mouth of the River Fleet.[316] In the early nineteenth century it had seven employees, but by 1889 only one; by 1893 it seems to have moved to Garlieston, and after that there is no further mention of it in *Trades Directories*.

It has been commented that Wigtown's failure to develop as a trading port in the nineteenth century was perhaps a result of a lack of ambition among a conservative merchant community. This may be true, but may demonstrate a realistic view of the potential profit balanced against the cost of harbour improvements and maintenance, and the practical problems of a river-mouth harbour within a sandy estuary.[317] On the other hand, the burgh never seems to have enjoyed the services of a visionary or dynamic provost or councillors, like the Maitland brothers at Tain, whose energy in business and local development transformed their community.[318] This was perhaps compounded by the fact that Wigtown shared an MP with three other Galloway burghs (**map 7**) – New Galloway, Stranraer and Whithorn – and while its voice was strong because the effective patronage of both Wigtown and Whithorn lay in the hands of the Earl of Galloway, it was Stranraer which attracted most investment due to its developing importance as a ferry port and, later, railway terminus. The position was further compounded after

Table 4 Occupational data from *OSA* and *Trades Directories*

Directories **Wigtown (burgh)**	*OSA* parish	1825	1837	1852	1867	1873	1878	1882	1886	1889	1893	1900	1903	1907	1911	1915
Resident gentry		7	7	13	30	16	21	22	26	x	18	10	10	21	19	16
Writers	5	6	9	9	7	7	5	4	5	7	9	8	8	8	5	5
Doctors	2	3	2	3	2	1	1	1	1	2	2	2	2	3	2	1
Vets					1	2	2	2	2	1	1	1	1	1	1	1
Banks, private		1	1													
British Linen			y	y	y	y	y	y	y	y	y	y	y	y	y	y
by 1861 City of Glasgow, 1878 National					y	y	y	y	y	y	y	y	y	y	y	y
1849 Edinburgh & Glasgow, 1858 Clydesdale (to 1942)				y	y	y	y	y	y	y	y	y	y	y	y	y
Hotels			1	1	2	2	2	2	2	2	2	2	1	2	3	3
King's/Queen's/Galloway Arms (now flats)				y c 1840	y	y	y	y	y	y	y	y	y	y	y	y
McDowall's 1834, Commercial 1963, County 2002 (Wigtown Ploughman) 30 South Main Street, 29 added 1941			y 1834	y	y	y	y	y	y	y	y	y	x	y	y	y
Temperance, Main Street															y	y
Booksellers/stationers/printers		2	2	3	4	3	3	4	6	4	4	2	1	2	1	1
Cattle-dealers					3	4	4	3	4	5	4	3	3	3	2	1
Tallow-chandlers		4			2	2	2	2	1	1	x	x	x	x	x	x
China-dealers							1	3	2	1	2	1	1	x	x	x
Innkeepers/vintners	6	10	1	3	4	5	6	6	6	6	6	6	5	6	5	3
Craig Inn, Agnew Crescent, demolished 1939				y		y	y	y	y	y	y	y	x	y	x	x
Ship				y												
Grapes, Agnew Crescent										y	y	y	y	y	y	y
Red Lion, Main Street			y (1820s)		y	y	y	y	y	y	y	y	y	y	y	y
Oriental, High Street											y	y	y	y	y	y
Masons, builders, wrights, plumbers	28		6	15	13	12	9	10	12	10	10	5	4	5	4	5
Saddlers		2			2	3	3	2	2	2	1	1	1	1	1	1
Manufacturer of preserved potato					y	x	y	y	y	y	y	y	y			
chemical manures									y	y	y	y	y	y	y	
Ship carpenter		1														
Ship owner/broker				1												
Seamen	12															
Customs House staff		6	4	4	2	1	2	2	2	1	1*	0				

*By 1893 the customs house seems to have moved to Garlieston, and by 1900 to have disappeared altogether, the role presumably joined with the general collection of revenue.

1885 when the burgh and county constituencies were merged, which diluted the town's voice still more. Wigtown's men of business would have had to lobby hard to secure their interests, but there is little evidence that the Earl of Galloway was active in their support. After all, he also had his own port of Garlieston to promote.

The one area where Wigtown's business remained robust was in the cattle trade, which was underpinned by the continued development of meat and dairy farming in the Machars in the first half of the nineteenth century. The importance of cattle to the local economy is indicated by the numbers of cattle-dealers and tallow-chandlers in the town (**table 4**), and in the *Trades Directories* for 1903 and 1907 an 'inspector of cattle sheds' was listed as a council employee. Wigtown's role as a regional market centre for local farmers was underscored by the establishment of an annual agricultural show, held in the great cattle park of South Field. Developed as part of that 'improving spirit' which had been commented on by observers since the late 1700s, shows of this kind were intended to promote improvement through competition between farmers for prizes for animals and other produce. This served to strengthen the area's reputation as a producer of high-quality cattle, but the security of the business which traded on that reputation needed more than 'best at show' rosettes to guarantee its future in a market where the introduction of refrigerated shipping from Argentina or Australia presented huge challenges. It was recognised, however, that the long-term success of the burgh as a centre of this trade depended on its communications links and, as railways spread into Galloway, rival centres like Castle Douglas and Newton Stewart had been quick to benefit. The major development with the greatest impact, therefore, was the arrival of the railway.

A line, mainly locally financed, had been built in 1859 from Dumfries to Castle Douglas, and continued to Portpatrick two years later, with branch lines to Stranraer completed in 1863, and to Kirkcudbright in 1864. In 1871 a public meeting was held in Newton Stewart to discuss building a line to Whithorn, with the lead being taken by Lord Garlies, heir to the Earl of Galloway. Following that, the Wigtownshire Railway Company was formed. Although not all the shares had been sold, it was agreed to begin work on the first section, which was easier in engineering terms, and in 1875 the line was opened to Wigtown.[319] The last line to be built in Galloway, the Wigtownshire Railway 'presents a particularly interesting example of a branch line constructed and operated almost entirely on local capital and initiative' and 'provides an interesting case-study of the effects of railway development in an isolated agricultural district, which traditionally relied on sea links'.[320] It was an optimistic operation but the line was barely profitable, and in 1885 the company merged with the Portpatrick railway and operations were taken over by the Glasgow and South-Western Railway. As a later generation in Wigtown saw it, 'Though hailed as a sign of renewed prosperity, this new

FIGURE 17

The old and new market
crosses (Volkmar Nix)

transport in fact brought about the downfall of the harbour' and eventually a decline in the local population.[321]

It was also hoped that the railway would help to bring in visitors, given the growing trend for touring holidays in nineteenth-century Scotland. Galloway generally had not attracted many visitors in the later eighteenth and early nineteenth century. With the exception of Bishop Pococke, none of the best-known travel writers, whose works did much to encourage others, such as Thomas Pennant, the Wordsworths or Coleridge, visited the area. By the 1830s Sir Walter Scott's novels had succeeded in boosting tourist traffic to the Highlands, the Trossachs and the eastern Borders, but, despite the success of his *Redgauntlet* or *The Bride of Lammermuir*, large parts of which had south-western settings, including Baldoon Castle, very close to Wigtown, there was no similar interest generated in visiting the region. What tourism there was appears to have been very limited and local. The arrival of the railway in 1875 stimulated the change of name of the Queen's Arms to the Galloway Arms, under new ownership, and by the 1890s this and the Commercial Inn were the burgh's main hotels.[322] However, they seem to have been patronised principally by commercial travellers and dealers rather than tourists.

While a trade-based recovery may have failed to materialise, the evidence for some degree of local prosperity that had become apparent in the late eighteenth century continued into the second quarter of the nineteenth century. In 1839 it was reported that the town had 'undergone great improvements within the last twenty years'; 'many new houses have been built, and a large space of an oblong figure, in the middle of the principal

FIGURE 18
County Buildings, 1862–63,
soon after refurbishment: an
impressive building, but out
of scale with the rest of the
town (Volkmar Nix)

FIGURE 19
County Buildings seen from
Windy Hill (Paula Martin)

street, which is unusually wide, had been enclosed, and planted with shrubs, evergreens, and forest trees. There are spacious gravel walks in it, and a bowling-green in the centre'.[323] The square, first laid out in 1809, remained a distinguishing feature, described as 'altogether a wonderfully fine thing, and quite unexampled in Scotland'.[324] The north side was altered in the 1840s when the new main road from the north was built,[325] and there was a further remodelling in 1887 occasioned by a dispute with the bowling club over the mature trees which shadowed the area.[326] These changes had, by the 1890s, produced the present form of a central rectangle of one acre, with trees, gravelled walks and bowling green, surrounded by railings. In the centre [of the west end] of the enclosed area stood the old and new burgh crosses (**fig 17**).[327] This central zone was further improved when a Gas Company was established in 1846, and the following year the streets were lit by gas.[328] A further manifestation of a greater self-consciousness in the burgh's appearance and its heritage can perhaps be seen in the Covenanters Monument, a great obelisk designed by James Maclaren, and built in 1858 by public subscription, at a cost of £200. It was erected on Windy Hill, so that it could be seen by visitors approaching the town (**fig 11**).[329]

There had also been piecemeal extensions to the late eighteenth-century tolbooth and council buildings, culminating in 1856 when a Telegraph House was built on the east side of the old building. Its upstairs room was used as a Council Chamber, replacing the smaller chamber in the town hall.[330] The next step in the improvement of the town centre came in 1862–63 when this apparently rambling complex was swept away and a new County Buildings and Town Hall were built (**figs 18 & 19**).[331]

> Forming the chief architectural ornament of the burgh, the County Buildings stand at the western end of the Square and occupy the site of an older building of the same nature erected in 1756. This fine Tudor structure … contains a court-room with the usual side rooms, the offices of the sheriff clerk, the public library and a large assembly hall. On the sides of the main entrance the arms of Stranraer and Whithorn are carved and the initial letters of the other principal places of the county appear on the keystones of the arched windows. Over the side entrance is an imperfect representation of the burgh arms, and on the wall to the left is a slab with the royal arms, taken from the court-house that formerly stood there. The tower belonging to the old building has been faced with new stonework, but the old Tolbooth beneath it has been preserved intact with its iron door and massive bolts. In the Council Chamber are to be seen the capacious [wooden] punch-bowl presented to the burgh by Queen Anne, a wooden drinking cup, five infitting beakers, a wine gallon, a quart, six bell-shaped and two circular weights, a three-legged bushel measure and other interesting relics. In the tower hang three bells dated respectively 1633, 1777 and 1881.[332]

Later it was suggested that the old tower had 'lost all architectural interest by being faced by new stonework', though it had retained the cell where the Wigtown Martyrs had, according to tradition, been held.[333] It had, however, long ceased to serve as the town jail. In 1839 the minister commented that 'The prison has long been complained of as insecure and unhealthy',[334] and this was replaced in 1846–48 by a new prison, 'outside the town, facing the south' (**fig 20**). When this became redundant in 1881 it was converted for use as a police station.[335]

Amidst the general improvement of the burgh's physical appearance in the

FIGURE 20
The prison, built 1846–48.
The central chimney stack
drew stale air from the cells,
a feature which prompted
the Jacobean gothic style
often seen in prisons
(Colin Martin)

first half of the nineteenth century, the one major building which remained in poor condition was the parish church. At a time when more-prosperous burghs were replacing their medieval kirks with new structures purpose-built for Presbyterian worship, Wigtown simply made do with a further patching-up of the old building. The old church had been re-roofed in 1831 but had been finally abandoned two decades later. By 1839, about 240 families were attending the established church,[336] emphasising how crowded the old building had become, and even the introduction of galleries could not ease pressure. Once abandoned, the old building quickly fell into ruin and by the end of the century was already reduced more or less to the condition in which it now stands, with only a portion of the south wall and east gable remaining.[337] Its replacement, completed in 1851, was described at the time as 'handsome', though is less attractive to modern eyes (**fig 21**).[338] The Earl of Galloway, who as the largest heritor bore the major part of the cost, 'generously presented the two beautiful windows that adorn the north and south gables, and gave two of the three stained glass windows erected in 1866 to the memory of the Rev Peter Young, who ministered in Wigtown for 65 years'. A pipe organ was introduced in 1877.[339]

The second half of the nineteenth century, as in most towns, saw a proliferation of church buildings following the various secessions from the Church of Scotland. A Free Church was built in Harbour Road in 1843–44, with 400 sittings, described as 'outwardly unpretentious in style, yet very tidy and snug internally'.[340] In 1845 the old Anti-Burgher meeting house was demolished and a new, 'unpretentious' United Secession church built, with 700 sittings, marking a significant rise from the 66 families noted in 1839 as forming part of the Seceding and Dissenting congregations. While there had been only 25 Roman Catholic families in the parish in 1839, over the next 40 years the immigration of Irish Catholics swelled that number and the church of the Sacred Heart, on South Main Street, the first Roman Catholic church in the Machars, was built in 1879. In 1900 the Free Church merged with the United Presbyterian church to form the United Free Church, and the congregation used the existing UP church, with the former Free Church as a hall. At the end of the nineteenth century there were four churches in the town, plus two sects of Plymouth Brethren, who had ceased to meet before the First World War.[341]

With the proliferation of churches there also came both rebuilding of schools and an increase in their number. In 1839 it was reported that there was 'an excellent grammar-school … conducted by an able teacher and assistant', teaching English, Latin, Greek, French, writing, arithmetic, book-keeping, and mathematics. 'Besides the public schools, there are two unendowed schools, whose teachers depend upon the school fees. There are also two Sunday schools, attended by nearly 300 children. The total number of scholars attending schools in the parish is about 450'.[342] A new parish/burgh school was built in 1845 at Lochan Croft and rebuilt in 1910 fronting onto New Road,[343] followed before 1867 by a new Charity School.[344] With

FIGURE 21
The new church, built in
1851 (Colin Martin)

FIGURE 22
Barbadoes Villa (1833–35)
(Richard Oram)

education linked directly to religion, the Free Church provided its own school, which was built in 1844 in Harbour Road (Dunmore House), near the prison. In 1889 it became a private girls' school.[345] All Souls Roman Catholic school, in New Road, was built in the late nineteenth century, with later additions. In 1873, when the first School Board was elected, there were six schools in the town, all fee-paying, but they gradually closed or amalgamated. In 1895 a secondary department was established in the burgh school.[346]

Private houses continued to be built or rebuilt. The Maclellan brothers, who set up the distillery at Bladnoch, lived in Wigtown in one of the big

FIGURE 23
The fine early eighteenth-century walled garden of Bank House: left, the gate in the south wall, looking south (Colin Martin); right, one of the garden pavilions, looking south-east (Paula Martin)

houses. One of them built Orchardton House, Acre Place, in 1827, and at about the same date Beechwood House was built below Acre Place for a customs official.[347] In 1833–35 Barbadoes Villa (later Dunure) was built on the southern edge of the town by a retired colonial (**fig 22**).[348] Woodside, Bladnoch Road, was built in 1836.[349] One of the grandest surviving houses is the former British Linen Bank, in Bank Street, built *c* 1840 of red sandstone and standing in an eighteenth-century walled garden with gate piers and square corner pavilions (**figs 23 & 24**);[350] No 11 Bank Street is also dated 1840. Many of the houses in Main Street probably date from between *c* 1750 and the first quarter of the nineteenth century.[351] In 1891 the burgh had 369 inhabited houses and 45 vacant, and by around the same date it was said that 'As seen from a distance the town presents a very picturesque appearance; and its neatness, cleanliness, and general air of comfort and good taste favourably impress those who enter it. The houses are built in a great diversity of styles, which lends an air of quaint variety to the principal streets; while some of the more recent edifices attain a very considerable degree of elegance'.[352] Another source said that the town 'presents a fine appearance from the railway and sea, being perched on an eminence. Wigtown is well arranged, and contains a beautiful central square, laid out in flower gardens, tennis courts, and promenades'.[353]

These various developments occurred against a background of rising population and changing demographic profile. Between 1801 and 1851 the

FIGURE 24
Bank House later became the
Wigtown House Hotel
(Mark Watson)

population of the parish increased by 92%. Later observers attributed much of this increase to improved trade, one commenting that, 'The new harbour was opened in 1817, and during the next 50 years Wigtown flourished as never before'.[354] In 1839 the minister claimed that 'The condition of the people has been greatly improved since the time of the last *Statistical Account*. They are now more cleanly in their habits, more comfortably lodged, and in consequence of a more easy communication, and of a more frequent intercourse with other districts of the country, both their diet and their dress are of a better description'.[355]

A major change in the population profile of the parish began with the steady increase in Irish immigration into Scotland after *c* 1790, but particularly after *c* 1815 and into the early 1850s.[356] Originating as a seasonal movement of agricultural labourers, mainly harvest-workers, the migrants began to put down roots in south-western Scotland and established a distinct community. At first, these economic migrants did not move far beyond their point of arrival, which provoked a series of social and economic problems in Galloway. Later many went further and moved into industrial work, seeking employment in factories in Glasgow, Paisley, and as far as Dundee. In 1839 the minister wrote that 'The great influx of Irish labourers and vagrants into this district operates heavily upon the poor's funds, and there is little prospect of that evil being corrected, while there is no legal provision for the indigent in that country'.[357]

In 1844 the minister reported that the great majority of the poor of the parish 'are Irish, or descended from parents who came from Ireland'. Most lived in the town, and most were Catholics.[358] The majority were from Ulster, and there were also significant numbers, perhaps about 25%, of Protestants. They brought with them several Ulster-Scots cultural institutions, even those of quite recent origin in the Irish troubles of the 1790s, such as the Loyal Orange Order.[359] The first Orange Lodge was established in Scotland in 1800 in Maybole, and by the 1830s there were Lodges in Wigtown, Kirkcudbright, Newton Stewart and Whithorn, as well as Glasgow and Paisley.[360] 'For troops, goods, Irish cattle, or Irish vagrants the south-west was a staging-post. To contemporaries the problems they brought in their passage through the region were often more evident than the benefits'.[361] While the large numbers may have been more perceived than real, it is certainly true that the Irish migrants were very poor. The south-west of Scotland was not a preferred destination, but it was the nearest and therefore the cheapest.[362] The introduction of steamships meant that immigrants could travel direct to Glasgow, instead of landing in Ayrshire or Galloway, and led to a falling away of immigration into Galloway from the middle of the century. Those who settled soon merged with the native population so that by the mid-twentieth century their descendants could not be 'distinguished from the other inhabitants by speech, condition or behaviour'.[363]

As well as Irish immigration, however, the burgh, like most places in

Table 5 Nineteenth-century adult deaths, by decade (from graveyard inscriptions)

			1800–09	1810–19	1820–29	1830–39	1840–49	1850–59	1860-69	1870–79	1880–89	1890–99	1900–09
Unpecified			33	33	56	77	113	110	105	104	107	55	41
Scotland	Galloway	Wigtown	2	1	4	3	10	11	22	17	25	44	26
		Bladnoch					1	1	6	6	7	7	5
		elsewhere		1		3	6	8	16	19	22	25	20
	various			1	1		3	5	1	3	9	5	6
England	various				1	1	2	5	7	3	4	7	4
		Liverpool						1	1	7	7	5	1
Ireland			1		1	1		1	1			2	
Europe			1					1				3	
USA				1	2	1	2	1	1	1	1	4	
Canada						1		1		1			
W Indies			1	2	1	1	1	3	1				
S America					1				1				
India and Far East						1	3	4	3			1	
Africa									1	1	3		1
Australia and New Zealand								2	1	7	3	2	2
At sea				1	1	2		1	1	2	2	1	1
Total			38	40	68	91	141	155	168	171	190	161	107

Scotland, experienced an exodus to the colonies. The surviving graveyard inscriptions record too few occupational descriptions to have any statistical validity, but they do frequently record the place of death. This is shown in **table 5**, and shows links with the West Indies from the later eighteenth century, tailing off by the 1860s. Links with the USA and Canada cover most of the century, while deaths in Australia and New Zealand peaked in the 1870s. There was also a growing exodus to other parts of Galloway, other parts of Scotland, and England. The English links were predominantly with Liverpool, and the majority of the others with the northern half of the country (perhaps symbolised by the naming of the house at the top of Harbour Road 'Rochdale').

Unlike other county towns, there is little evidence at Wigtown for a thriving social life and community spirit as manifested in societies and associations, social, cultural, educational or business, presumably because the population was so small. There was a Mechanics Institute, and a Friendly Society, which had been established in 1795, and 'encourages a spirit of independence, and stimulates to industry, and prevents many from becoming a burden upon the community'.[364] A document compiled in 1857 lists those who were members between 1846 and 1850 and how much they were paid, or what happened to them. The 51 members consisted of 13 farmers, 8 labourers, 6 joiners, 5 merchants, 3 smiths, 3 watchmakers, 2 tailors, and one each of brickmaker, carrier, carter, cooper, innkeeper, mason, mole-catcher, nailer, sailor, seaman, and shoemaker.[365] A branch of the Oddfellows was established in 1873, and a lodge of freemasons started in 1903. There had been a masonic lodge at the time of the erection of the new Mercat Cross, with a lodge in Agnew Crescent, but it had clearly died out.[366] The Wigtown Bowling Club was founded in 1830, one of the earliest in Scotland.[367] There was not, however, despite the local influence of Peter M'Kerlie, much involvement in the Dumfriesshire and Galloway Natural History and Antiquarian Society, and no development of a Wigtownshire museum to match that founded for the Stewartry in Kirkcudbright.

It was not just within the burgh that the population had expanded. In Bladnoch, at the beginning of the nineteenth century, 'there were only ten or twelve old thatched cottages on both sides of the road, tenanted by the labouring classes', and the public house at the bridge-end.[368] This situation changed dramatically in the middle of the century, triggered in 1867 by the building of a new bridge over the Bladnoch, by D & T Stevenson.[369] By the 1870s the village consisted of 30 or 40 houses, all with slate roofs, some of them two storeys high. As well as Maclellan's Distillery, there was 'Mr George Maclellan's extensive Patent Preserved Potato and Farina Mill at Fordbank', a coach-builder, an iron foundry, as well as shops and workshops.[370]

1914 to the present

Like most communities in Britain, Wigtown's experience of the wars and social upheavals of the twentieth century was traumatic. It lost 54 of its young men in the First World War, representing a significant percentage of its workforce. These losses were commemorated on the war memorial erected beside the church, to which later were added the names of a further fourteen men killed in the Second World War.[371] The wars, however, were mainly a remote experience, although in 1939–45 the aerodrome at Baldoon (OS grid NX433 533) was important for the training of navigators. There were up to 200 men in camps in the area,[372] which brought a significant influx of much-needed investment. In Wigtown, there was a Land Army Hostel in Kirkland Terrace, and a canteen for the Baldoon airmen in Agnew Crescent.[373] Generally, however, the town was too distant from the main training areas south of Garlieston where the D-Day landings were rehearsed and, when the war ended, there was a rapid running down of the military facilities in the area, further fuelling the major problem faced by the district: unemployment.

The twentieth century saw continuing large-scale social and economic change which had a wide range of impacts, positive and negative, on the burgh. Some of the most far-reaching effects were triggered by changes in the rural economy, the structure of the rural labour-force, and the pattern of landholding. Soon after 1918 the Earl of Galloway disposed of his land in the parish, ending his family's four centuries of dominance of the district. Most of the former tenant-farmers became proprietors.[374] In the mid-twentieth century farming was seen, as always, to be the 'strong and firm basis on which the county economy is built' and to have been in particularly good health. It was recognised that dairying had fallen on 'evil days' in the 1920s but had been rescued by the establishment of the Milk Marketing Boards in 1933. The Bladnoch Creamery, which had opened in 1899, was taken over by the Scottish Wholesale Co-operative Society and employed 92 people at its peak in the 1950s. Arable cultivation had also done well during the war years and, from the later nineteenth century, had benefited from the purchase of local barley by the distillery. For a while there was a potato-preserving factory, but it had closed by the 1950s.[375] The uncertainties of the market for agricultural produce had its own impact on employment, but one of the biggest shifts came about through the progressive expansion of mechanisation in farming. Between 1945 and 1955 horses were generally replaced by tractors,[376] removing the demand for large numbers of farmworkers to handle plough-teams.

The port, too, had finally failed. In 1959 it was reported that 'the harbour is forlorn and derelict but the town has other industries and outlets for its trade and talents'.[377] There were, despite that optimistic observation, few other local sources of employment, reflected in the closure of all but one of the town's banks by 1959. Workers had to travel out of the Wigtown area to, for example, the woollen mill at Newton Stewart or the expanding forestry plantations in the north of the county, while some employment was also provided in road maintenance and railways (although the line to Wigtown itself closed in 1950), and the buses, which experienced great expansion in the post-1945 period. Employment opportunities in Galloway as a whole were still few and by the 1950s it was recognised that many young people were having to leave the district to find permanent jobs. Even before the 1960s it was observed that this exodus was only partly offset by migration into the district, and Wigtown in particular, with most of the new arrivals being retirees.[378] The profile of the population was beginning to change markedly.

These changes in the character of the burgh were also reflected in alterations to its legal and parliamentary status. After 1918 the parliamentary constituencies of Wigtownshire and Kirkcudbrightshire were merged into a single Galloway constituency. At one time county council meetings alternated between Wigtown and Stranraer, but by the 1950s they were held regularly in premises acquired for the purpose in Stranraer. In 1948 one police force was created for the whole of Dumfries and Galloway, replacing two county forces and a burgh force in Dumfries. The headquarters was in Dumfries, with sub-divisions in Kirkcudbright, Newton Stewart and Stranraer. Wigtown, however, did retain its sheriff court until 1975, held alternately there and in Stranraer; the district court last met in 1998.[379]

At the start of the twentieth century, formal religion still played a major part in the lives of most Scots. The prominence of church-going meant that church enlargement was one of the few significant projects to be undertaken. Extensive alterations to the parish church were begun in 1914 and, after being interrupted by the war, were completed in 1925. Ten years later the church hall was built for work among the young and for other social and religious activities. It also served for some years as an unofficial cinema for films used for religious instruction.[380] Declining population, coupled with a trend of falling church attendance, saw the number of churches gradually decrease. By the late 1940s there was only the parish church and the Roman Catholic church, with the old UP church becoming the west church, but in 1948 it, too, united with the parish church.[381] There were changes, too, in education, which in 1919 had become the responsibility of the county council. School provision from 1935 was gradually centralised, with the main secondary school in the area being Douglas Ewart in Newton Stewart, which became comprehensive in 1956. Wigtown school retained infant and primary classes, and a junior secondary department offering domestic science for girls and technical subjects for boys. The Roman Catholic primary school survived into the 1960s.[382]

Although Wigtown's population was declining, the first steps were being taken to improve the standards of housing for working families in the town. In the 1930s the first council housing was provided, in Lightlands Terrace and Lightlands Avenue, followed by New Road and Fountainblue, Jubilee, renovated cottages at Smith Terrace, Lilico Loaning and Seaview. By 1963 the council had rehoused 124 families. In the 1960s and 1970s council flats and houses were built in High Street, North Main Street, Chapel Court, Agnew Crescent, Lochancroft Lane and New Road, and the development at Seaview was completed.[383] After a fire in the 1980s the Galloway Inn was rebuilt as flats.[384] Another significant area of improvement was in water supply and sanitation. In the early 1900s the burgh's water supply was described as 'inadequate and bad: all but the fortunate few who had private wells had to depend on rain water collected in barrels or water drawn from street pumps, some of which was unfit for domestic purposes or even contaminated from the sewers', but not enough people were prepared to share the cost of bringing water 11 miles (18km) from Cairnsmore. It was 1930 before this was achieved. With it came better sewerage, and also a council-provided scavenging service. By the 1960s there were plans for further improving the water supply. Domestic and public gas-use for heating, cooking and lighting also developed when the private gas company was taken over by the town council in *c* 1920 and nationalised in 1948, though the town gas works closed in 1955. Energy provision by then had largely been taken over by electricity, following the 1931 establishment of the Wigtownshire Electricity Company.[385] By 1959, it was claimed that 'Wigtown, with its modern sanitation, its wide and well lit streets, and a good water supply, is a delightful place to live in and any house offered for sale finds a ready buyer'.[386]

The Square was still an impressive centre to the town, but had undergone several changes to its appearance by 1959. It was commented that 'the beauty of the scene has been marred, and the Square given a bare appearance, by the cutting down of the tall and stately chestnut trees that formerly graced it'.[387] When the public tennis courts at its eastern end fell into disuse in more recent times they were replaced by planting, walks and benches.[388] The area had retained a certain symbolism to the community as a place of public assembly into the second quarter of the twentieth century. It was there, for example, that the 'loyal inhabitants were wont to assemble in the Square once a year to drink from the town's large punch-bowl to the health of the reigning sovereign', but this practice had been less regular even by the late 1800s. The bowl was last used for such a public occasion on 20 May 1931, when the new water supply was turned on.[389] A continued sense of community in a public event remained with the Wigtown Show, held on the first Wednesday in August in the South Field, while a greater sense of tradition was offered by the revival of the Riding of the Marches in a fashion similar to that of the Border burghs after the Second World War.[390] While facilities like the tennis courts eventually fell entirely into disuse in the later twentieth century, other council-established facilities, such as the golf course founded in 1959, flourished.[391] Some societies such as the choral society were short-lived, but others continued to thrive.

The long slump in the town's fortunes which seemed to have accelerated post-1945 had a generally negative impact on the physical condition of the community. There was little inward investment to attract significant employers and, with the accelerating recession of the rural economy in the later 1980s several local companies closed. The result was a further decline in population. There was perhaps a certain symbolism in the infilling in the 1970s of the old harbour with debris including the demolished buildings from Baldoon airfield.

Soon after, however, plans were instituted to capitalise on the rich heritage of the burgh and its environs, which began with better signposting of sites and visitor attractions and the development of trails around the town. These led visitors to the supposed site of the Martyrs' drowning near the pre-nineteenth-century harbour site and, following the disused railway line, round to the castle site. The rich natural heritage of the district has also been recognised as a major tourist draw, with trails and hides being established at the mouth of the Bladnoch. Less than 20 years after the harbour site had been infilled, the main section of quayside and dock was tidied up and can now be used by small boats.[392] The town itself has been given a new sense of energy by the promotion of Wigtown as 'Scotland's Book Town' in 1997. Coupled with a recent Townscape Heritage Initiative, which resulted in substantial cosmetic improvements to the area around North and South Main Street, this status has significantly boosted both the economy and the appearance of the town. There is once again an air of prosperity and optimism, and the town has retained its individual character.

Notes

1   NMRS record NX45SW 10.

2   G Wilson, 'Notice of a collection of implements of stone and bronze, now presented to the museum, and exhibited to the meeting, and other Antiquities from Wigtownshire', *PSAS* **14** (1879–80), 126–7; NMRS record NX45NW 12.

3   *Catalogue of the National Museum of Antiquities of Scotland* (new edn, Edinburgh, 1892); F E S Roe, 'The battle-axes, mace-heads and axe-hammers from south-west Scotland', *TDGNHAS*, 3rd ser **44** (1967), 80; NMRS record NX45NW 11.

4   T H McK Clough and W A Cummins, 'Lists of identifications', in Clough and Cummins, *Stone axe studies, volume 2: the petrology of prehistoric stone implements from the British Isles* (CBA Res Rep **67**, London 1988), 242, nos. WIG 102, 104.

5   H E Maxwell, 'Ancient weapons, instruments, utensils and ornaments of Wigtonshire. With list of the principal stone implements recorded from Wigtonshire', *Archaeol Hist Collect Ayrshire Galloway* **5** (1885), 51.

6   W F Cormack, 'Wigtown, Roman coin', *DES 1967*, 55; NMRS record NX45NW 8.

7   A Haggarty and G Haggarty, 'Excavations at Rispain Camp, Whithorn, 1978–81', *TDGNHAS*, 3rd ser **58** (1985), 21–51.

8   W G Collingwood, 'The Early Crosses of Galloway', *TDGNHAS* 3rd ser **10** (1922–23), 221–3.

9   Symson, *Large Description of Galloway*, 34; NMRS records NX45NW 37 & 44 [wrong grid ref].

10 T S Muir, *Ecclesiological Notes on some of the Islands of Scotland* (Edinburgh, 1885), 245.

11 NMRS record NX45NW 4.

12 NMRS record NX45NW 4.

13 A E Truckell and J Williams, 'Mediaeval pottery in Dumfriesshire and Galloway', *TDGNHAS*, 3rd ser **44** (1966–67), 133.

14 M'Kerlie, *Lands and their Owners*, 151; R C Reid, 'Some notes on pre-Reformation Wigtown', *TDGNHAS*, 3rd ser **12** (1924–25), 241–2; NMRS record NX45NW 2.

15 Scheduled Ancient Monument No 11055.

16 NMRS records NX45NW 17–18.

17 *Burgh of Wigtown, Official Guide* (Croydon, [1959]), 12.

18 G Fraser, *Wigtown and Whithorn: Historical and Descriptive Sketches, Stories and Anecdotes, Illustrative of the Racy Wit and Pawky Humour of the District* (Wigtown, 1877), 24.

19 Symson, in Macfarlane, *Geographical Collections*, **ii**, 74.

20 M'Kerlie, *Lands and their Owners,* 153–4.

21 NMRS record NX45NW 5 at NX 4365 5552 (OS visit 17 Sept 1970); OS 1848 Town Plan of Wigtown; NMRS record NX45NW 60.

22 NMRS record NX45NW 59 at NX 4366 5561.

23 M'Kerlie, *Lands and their Owners*, 153; NMRS record NX45NW 14.

24 19 Bank Street, former Wigtown House Hotel. Local informants suggested NX 435 554; NMRS record NX45NW 5.

25 NMRS record NX45NW 5.

26 J Brann, 'Harbour Road, Wigtown, Dumfries and Galloway (Wigtown parish), wall', *DES 2001*, 28; NMRS record NX45NW 68.

27 M Noel, 'Black's Field, Wigtown (Wigtown parish), geophysical survey', *DES 2003*, 52.

28 G Fraser, *Lowland Lore; or the Wigtownshire of long ago* (Wigtown, 1880), 35.

29 Identified by R B K Stevenson, NMAS, 1970; NMRS record NX45NW 10.

30 J Brann, '11 North Main Street, Wigtown, Dumfries and Galloway (Wigtown parish), laird's town house', *DES 2001*, 29; NMRS record NX45NW 69; Listed Grade B (HB No 42404).

31 W F Cormack, 'Wigtown burgh and parish 10 North Bank Street, inscribed and carved stones', *DES 1983*, 4; NMRS record NX45NW 19.

32 V Nix, '17 Agnew Crescent, Wigtown, Dumfries and Galloway (Wigtown parish), sculptured panel', *DES 2001*, 28; NMRS record NX45NW 67.01.

33 J Brann, '26 South Main Street, Wigtown (Wigtown parish), medieval burgh watching brief', *DES 1997*, 27; NMRS record NX45NW 23.01.

34 D Hall, 'High Vennel, Wigtown (Wigtown parish)', *DES 1992*, 27; NMRS record NX45NW 49.

35 Information from Dumfries and Galloway SMR.

36 J Brann, 'Wigtown, Dumfries and Galloway (Wigtown parish), watching briefs', *DES 2000*, 23; NMRS record NX45NW 63.

37 Brann, *DES 2000*, 23; NMRS record NX45NW 64.

38 Information from Dumfries and Galloway SMR, 2006.

39 *The Dublin guild merchant roll, c 1190–1265,* eds P Connolly and G Martin (Dublin, 1992), the men were Michael Ruffus and Peter Longus; Dublin, City Archives, 1/1, 2m.20a; 1/1, 2m.30b.

40 R D Oram, 'Dervorgilla, the Balliols and Buittle', *TDGNHAS*, 3rd ser **73** (1999), 169.

41 A A M Duncan, *Scotland: the Making of the Kingdom* (Edinburgh, 1975), 531.

42 R D Oram, *The Lordship of Galloway* (Edinburgh, 2000), 152.

43 *The Exchequer Rolls of Scotland*, ed J Stuart *et al* (Edinburgh, 1878–1908), **i**, 30–1, by 'master Peter the mason'.

44   *Wigtownshire Charters*, ed R C Reid (SHS, 1960), **xli** n.3.

45   *Wigtownshire Chrs*, **xli** n.3.

46   *ER*, **i**, 22.

47   R D Oram, P F Martin, C A McKean, and S Anderson, *Historic Whithorn: Archaeology and Development* (CBA, York, 2010).

48   *ER*, **i**, 39.

49   *Calendar of Documents Relating to Scotland,* ed J Bain (4 vols, Edinburgh, 1881–88), **ii**, 1272–1307, nos 520, 547, 550.

50   *CDS*, **ii**, nos 572–4; *Documents Illustrative of the History of Scotland 1286–1306*, ed J Stevenson (Edinburgh, 1870), **i**, 278–9, Doc CCVIII.

51   *CDS*, **ii**, nos 582, 589.

52   *Rotuli Scotiae in Turri Londiniensi et in Domo Capitulari Westmonasteriensi Asservati*, eds D Macpherson *et al*, 2 vols (London, 1814–19), **i**, 31a.

53   *Rot. Scot.*, **i**, 46a, 47a.

54   W Rishanger, *Chronica et Annales*, ed H T Riley (London: Rolls Ser, 1865), 440–6. For English losses at the Cree, see *Liber Quotidianus Contrarotulatoris Garderobae Anno Regni Edwardi Primi Vicesimo Octavo*, ed J Topham (London, 1787), 175, 185.

55   The Comyns were evidently in control of Galloway from at least summer 1297 until at least 1301, when Edward, Prince of Wales, planned to make a pilgrimage to Whithorn.

56   *CDS*, **ii**, 443, James Alilegh and John Weston.

57   M'Kerlie, *Lands and their Owners,* 151; *NSA*, 2, in 1839 'the fosse is quite discernable'.

58   See entry in *Oxford Dictionary of National Biography*, http://www.oxforddnb.com/, his wife had been nurse to the infant Prince David.

59   *Regesta Regum Scotorum*, **vi**, *The Acts of David II*, ed B Webster (Edinburgh, 1976), nos 25, 27, 30, 31, 33, 35, 483, where Malcolm is a witness to David's charters issued during this period.

60   *RRS*, **vi**, no 39.

61   See 'The forfeited estates of the Black Douglases' in P G B McNeill and H L MacQueen eds, *Atlas of Scottish History to 1707* (Edinburgh, 1996), 447. The properties which seem to have had Wigtown as their focus were Baldoon, Barglass, Barnbarroch, Blairmaken, Clauchrie, Clutag, Corwar, Eggerness, Killadam, Kildarroch, Kirbreen, Kirwaugh, Knockan, Knockefferick and Knockencur. Some were substantial properties, Baldoon and Barnbarroch, for example, becoming after 1455 the centres of important baronies held by the Dunbar and Vaus families, both very influential in Wigtown politics.

62   See for example *Wigtownshire Chrs*, no 37 for his grant of regality jurisdiction to the abbot of Glenluce. There is otherwise no evidence for an attempt to use local patronage to win a deeper reservoir of support.

63   M A Penman, *David II, 1329–71* (East Linton, 2004), 214 n.59, 244.

64   *Registrum Magni Sigilli Regum Scotorum*, **i**, *1306–1424*, ed J M Thomson (repr Edinburgh, 1984), no 250.

65   *RRS*, **vi**, no 451.

66   *RMS*, **i**, no 527.

67 *RMS*, **i**, no 414.

68 M Brown, *The Black Douglases: war and lordship in late Medieval Scotland, 1300–1455* (East Linton, 1998), 63–4.

69 It is probably in this role of court centre that Wigtown appears on 10 Nov 1427 (the date suggesting a Martinmas court diet) as the venue for the formal grant of lands, castle and constabulary of Lochnaw by James Douglas of Leswalt to Andrew Agnew (*Registrum Magni Sigilli Regum Scotorum*, **ii**, *1424–1513*, ed J Balfour Paul (repr Edinburgh, 1984), no 183; *Wigtownshire Chrs*, no 134).

70 Brown, *Black Douglases*, 117, 216.

71 *RMS*, **ii**, no 47.

72 Brown, *Black Douglases*, 240–1.

73 *Wigtownshire Chrs*, no 37.

74 The burgh's fairs were confirmed in 1662 as the 'Palme fair and Midsummer fair, Lammas and Martinmas fair' (*Registrum Magni Sigilli Regum Scotorum*, **xi**, no 243).

75 Brown, *Black Douglases*, 275.

76 Brown, *Black Douglases*, 288.

77 *RMS*, **ii**, no 503.

78 *Wigtownshire Chrs*, no 89; D Brooke, 'Wigtown: Profile of a Medieval Burgh', *TDGNHAS*, 3rd ser **60** (1985), 52–3.

79 *RMS*, **ii**, no 1143. Confirmed by the king and exempted from revocation on his attaining his perfect majority, 20 Feb 1478 (*RMS*, **ii**, no 1365).

80 *Wigtownshire Chrs*, no 90.

81 Brooke, 'Wigtown', 55–6.

82 *RMS*, **ii**, no 1624, in 1471 he received from Gilbert McDowell of Ravenstone the two merklands of Carseriggan in the north of Kirkcowan parish.

83 *RMS*, **ii**, no 1623. Interestingly, the lands were burdened, in addition to the rent of 12d per annum, with an obligation to provide the Abbot of Glenluce with pasture for one horse when he happened to come to Wigtown, an arrangement which suggests that the abbey did not possess any property in the burgh.

84 *RMS*, **ii**, no 2273; *RMS*, **ii**, no 2975 records the final sale of Kilsture and Claunch to Simon in 1506. Brooke, 'Wigtown', 55–6.

85 *ER*, **xi**, 62.

86 Brooke, 'Wigtown', 56–7.

87 Brooke, 'Wigtown', 58–60.

88 Royal Commission on the Ancient and Historical Monuments of Scotland, *Galloway vol i. Wigtownshire* (Edinburgh, 1912), 182. Machutus is also the dedicatory saint of Lesmahagow. An alternative identification with the Irish Mo-Cuta, Abbot of Lismore, has also been proposed (J Macqueen, 'The Gaelic speakers of Galloway and Carrick', *Scottish Studies* **xvii** (1973), 17–33), but the presence of another Welsh/Breton dedication, to Brioc or Brieuc, further east in coastal Galloway at Dunrod suggests that the Machutus/Malo identification cannot be dismissed. *RMS*, **ii**, no 1144. The cross-slab is now kept inside the church.

89 Surprisingly, however, despite this apparently free status, Wigtown is not listed in the rolls of the papal tax-collector, Master Boiamund di Vitia, 'Bagimond's Roll – Statement of the Tenths of the Kingdom of Scotland', ed A I Dunlop, *Miscellany of the Scottish History Society* **vi** (SHS, 1939), 3–77.

90 Oram, *Lordship of Galloway*, 149.

91 *CDS*, **iii**, no 69.

92 *Calendar of Documents Relating to Scotland*, **v**, *1108–1516* (Supplementary), eds G G Simpson and J D Galbraith (Edinburgh, 1985), no 653.

93 Edward Bruce's charter, which probably dated to *c* 1312–15, has not survived and the grant to Whithorn is known only from King Robert's subsequent general confirmation of 14th-century gifts in *RMS*, **i**, app i, no 20.

94 I B Cowan, *The Parishes of Medieval Scotland* (Scottish Record Society, 1967), 210.

95 *RMS*, **ii**, no 2273. In 1484, Master William was the notary public who recorded the grant of the lands of Monkhill to Simon McCristen (*RMS*, **ii**, no 1623). At the time of this grant, he had secured the vicarage of Penninghame.

96 *Wigtownshire Chrs*, nos 91, 93.

97 *Wigtownshire Chrs*, no 118.

98 NAS GD1/1110; NRAS 631/4/Bundle A950 no 36.

99 *RMS*, **iv**, no 2600.

100 NRAS 631/4/Bundle A950, no 20.

101 *Androw of Wyntoun's Orygynal Cronykil of Scotland*, ed A Laing (Edinburgh, 1872–79), Bk VIII, chap 8, lines 1514–16; I B Cowan, and D E Easson, *Medieval Religious Houses: Scotland*, 2nd edn (London, 1976), 121.

102 *Rot. Scot.*, **i**, 39b. A T Simpson and S Stevenson, *Historic Wigtown: the archaeological implications of development* (Scottish burgh survey ser, Glasgow, 1981), 7, were wrong in their reference to 1289/90 as the earliest date, which represents a misreading of their source.

103 NRAS 631/4/Bundle A950 no 6.

104 *ER*, **i**, 358–9.

105 *Accounts of the Lord High Treasurer of Scotland*, **ii**, 1500–1504, ed J Balfour Paul (Edinburgh, 1900), 81.

106 *TA*, **ii**, 249.

107 *TA*, **ii**, 264; *TA*, **iii**, 66, 287, 292.

108 *TA*, **iii**, 73.

109 *TA*, **iii**, 195, 376.

110 *TA*, **iii**, 274, 376.

111 *Registrum Secreti Sigilli Regum Scotorum*, eds M Livingstone *et al* (Edinburgh, 1882–1914), **ii**, no 4149; *Wigtownshire Chrs*, no 101.

112 Cowan and Easson, *Medieval Religious Houses*, 121.

113 *Wigtownshire Chrs*, no 107.

114 NAS GD10/554.

115 Eg NRAS 76/1/12, 24 Jul 1611.

116 *The Knights of St John of Jerusalem in Scotland*, eds I B Cowan, P H R Mackay and A Macquarrie (SHS, 1983), 18.

117 NRAS 76/1/37, 13 Mar 1629.

118   *Wigtownshire Chrs*, no 106.

119   *RPC*, **vii**, 381, 394, 670.

120   *RSS*, **ii**, no 1758.

121   *ER*, **i**, 316.

122   *ER*, **i**, 374.

123   Murray, 'Customs Accounts', 136.

124   Murray, 'Customs Accounts', 137–8.

125   *ER*, **iv**, 558.

126   *ER*, **vi**, 125.

127   Kirkcudbright's exports of raw wool declined to 3 sacks in 1469–71, falling to
      1 sack 16 stones by 1511 (*ER*, **viii**, 132; *ER*, **xiii**, 389).

128   *ER*, **vi**, 494–9; *ER*, **xiii**, 389.

129   *ER*, **xiii**, 389.

130   *ER*, **vi**, 125.

131   *ER*, **ix**, p lxx.

132   *ER*, **xiii**, 389.

133   Lindsay, *Rutter*, 53, 'Iff ye will lye at Wigtonne, pas north above the cost off
      Quhythyrne whill ye come to the mouth of Crey and ly ner to the toune in
      the mough of Blaidnoch'.

134   Murray, 'Customs Accounts', 146.

135   *Acts of the Lords of Council in Public Affairs 1501–1554: Selections from Acta
      Dominorum Concilii*, ed R K Hannay (Edinburgh, 1932), 314, 493.

136   *The Acts of the Lords Auditors of Causes and Complaints 1466–1494*, ed
      T Thomson (London, 1839), 122–3.

137   *ER*, **xiii**, 491.

138   A E Truckell, 'Wigtown Burgh Court Book, 1512–1535', *TDGNHAS*, 3rd ser
      62 (1987), 68.

139   Truckell, 'Wigtown Burgh Court Book', 68, on this occasion the wine was
      valued at 13 crowns the tun and the salt likewise. Again payment was to be
      one-third in silver and two-thirds in 'penworttis', divided equally between
      cloth and hides.

140   *Wigtownshire Chrs*, no 104.

141   *Wigtownshire Chrs*, no 109.

142   *Wigtownshire Chrs*, no 111.

143   *Wigtownshire Chrs*, no 110.

144   *Wigtownshire Chrs*, no 113. This was a re-issue of royal burgh status following
      the destruction of the Black Douglases and annexation of their estates to
      the crown in 1455. Wigtown had been granted to Malcolm Fleming as a
      component of his earldom of Wigtown by David II in 1341 (*RRS*, **vi**, no 39)
      and placed under his regality jurisdiction. The implication of this is that it
      had lost its 'royal' status, no longer being an immediate crown tenant, and
      that it had passed as a burgh in barony or regality from the Flemings to the
      Black Douglases with the earldom in the 1370s, a status confirmed by royal
      charter to William, 8th Earl of Douglas, in Oct 1451 (*RMS*, **ii**, no 503). As a
      consequence, earlier charters bestowing royal burgh status had presumably
      been cancelled and the new grant of royal burgh status gave Wigtown an

ancestry extending back only a little more than half a century at the date of their complaint.

145 *Wigtownshire Chrs*, no 114a.

146 *Wigtownshire Chrs*, no 94; *RMS*, **ii**, no 3401.

147 *Wigtownshire Chrs*, no 97.

148 *Wigtownshire Chrs*, no 95.

149 *Wigtownshire Chrs*, nos 96, 98–100.

150 *RSS*, **iv**, no 502. For Ahannay as provost see, *Wigtownshire Chrs*, 121.

151 *Wigtownshire Chrs*, 121.

152 Fraser, *Lowland Lore*, 18.

153 Fraser, *Lowland Lore*, 53.

154 See, for example, *Wigtownshire Chrs*, nos 41, 45, 47.

155 *Wigtownshire Chrs*, nos 52, 59, 67, 68, 69.

156 *Register of the Privy Council of Scotland*, eds J H Burton *et al* (Edinburgh, 1877–1970), **iv**, 612.

157 *RPC*, **vi**, *1599–1604*, ed D Masson (Edinburgh, 1884), 243, 262; NRAS 76/1/11.

158 *RPC*, **vi**, 243.

159 *RPC*, **vi**, 262.

160 *RPC*, **vi**, 306.

161 *RPC*, **vi**, 308.

162 *RPC* 3rd ser, **viii**, 381, 394.

163 *Registrum Magni Sigilli Regum Scotorum*, **vii**, no 1861, dated 9 Jul 1618.

164 C A Ralegh Radford and G Donaldson, *Whithorn and Kirkmadrine* (HMSO, 1953), 26.

165 *Third Statistical Account*, 392; RCAHMS Inventory of Monuments and Constructions in Galloway, vol.1, County of Wigtown (Edinburgh, 1912), 185.

166 F Dow, *Cromwellian Scotland 1651–1660* (Edinburgh, 1979), 42.

167 'Report by Thomas Tucker upon the Settlement of the Revenues of Excise and Customs in Scotland. AD MDCLVI', in *Miscellany of the Scottish Burgh Records Society* (Edinburgh, 1881), 28.

168 A Tayler and H Tayler, *John Graham of Claverhouse* (London, 1939), 40–1.

169 Tayler and Tayler, *Claverhouse*, 10, 14, 166.

170 Stell, *Dumfries and Galloway*, no 63.

171 *RMS*, **xi**, no 243.

172 This is a feature found in other such small burghs, for example Tain (R D Oram, P F Martin, C A McKean, A Cathcart, and T Neighbour, *Historic Tain: Archaeology and Development* (CBA, York, 2009)).

173 Fraser, *Lowland Lore*, 8.

174 Fraser, *Lowland Lore*, 3.

175 Fraser, *Lowland Lore*, 18. In 1686, the unnamed Irvine vessel carried barrelled herring, salt beef, dried fish, salt and tar; in 1687, the *Sibella* of Lochhead of Kintyre carried salt, butter, cheese and coals.

176 *RPC*, **x**, 137–8.

177 *RMS*, **vii**, no 231. One of the tenements had fallen to the king on account of the bastardy of its former possessor, William Vaus, but the others seem to have been left to fall vacant.

178 R D Oram, '"It cannot be decernit quha are clene and quha are foulle". Responses to epidemic disease in sixteenth- and seventeenth-century Scotland', *Renaissance and Reformation* **30**(4) (Centre for Reformation and Renaissance Studies, 2006).

179 Symson, *Large Description,* 34.

180 Fraser, *Wigtown and Whithorn*, 21; T C Smout, *Scottish Trade on the Eve of Union, 1660–1707* (Edinburgh, 1963), 77, 110.

181 Fraser, *Wigtown and Whithorn*, 21–2.

182 As the closest parallel is Dumfries, it may just be that the size of the market place was a regional feature.

183 M'Kerlie, *Lands and their Owners,* 159.

184 *RPC*, **v**, 505–6.

185 See Oram *et al*, *Whithorn*.

186 *A Tour through the whole Island of Great Britain,* eds G D H Cole and D C Browning (London, 1962), **ii**, 327.

187 Fraser, *Lowland Lore*, 3.

188 Smout, *Scottish Trade on the Eve of Union*, 148.

189 Fraser, *Lowland Lore*, 19.

190 Fraser, *Lowland Lore*, 4.

191 Symson, *Large Description,* 35–6.

192 Fraser, *Lowland Lore*, 13.

193 Fraser, *Lowland Lore*, 17.

194 Fraser, *Lowland Lore*, 18.

195 Fraser, *Lowland Lore*, 24.

196 M'Kerlie, *Lands and their Owners,* 159. It was quite normal for towns to be significantly in debt at this period, and was manageable provided there was enough income to pay the interest.

197 'Register Containing the State and Condition of every Burgh within the Kingdom of Scotland ... 1692', in *Miscellany of the Scottish Burgh Records Society* (Edinburgh, 1881), 108–9.

198 'Register Containing the State and Condition of every Burgh', 108–9.

199 Stell, *Dumfries and Galloway*, 69.

200 D Brewster, *Wigtown: the Story of a Royal and Ancient Burgh* (Newton Stewart, nd), 38.

201 Brewster, *Wigtown*, 41.

202 Fraser, *Wigtown and Whithorn*, 61. The combining of burgh and parish school was probably relatively common in small towns, and was certainly the case in Cupar (P Martin, *Cupar: the History of a Small Scottish Town* (Edinburgh, 2006), 175).

203 Fraser, *Lowland Lore*, 8–9.

204 See R D Oram, 'Abondance inépuisable? Crise de l'approvisionnement en combustible et réactions en Ecosse du Nord entre environ 1500 et environ 1800', in J-M Derex and F Gregoire, *Histoire économique et sociale de la tourbe et des tourbières*, Æstuaria: Cordemais, 2009, 31–44.

205 'Report by Thomas Tucker', 28; Fraser, *Lowland Lore*, 18.

206 Fraser, *Lowland Lore*, 12.

207 Fraser, *Lowland Lore*, 20.

208 Fraser, *Lowland Lore*, 24.

209 Fraser, *Lowland Lore*, 14, 16, 26, the problem continued into the 18th century (1702).

210 Fraser, *Lowland Lore*, 19, such problems may also have been associated with increasing urban density, as similar complaints can be found in other burghs, for example Cupar, during the 18th century (Martin, *Cupar*, 183).

211 Rupert Houseley's palaeoenvironmental analysis of Rispain Moss points to the systematic stripping of viably extractable peat supplies from the entire upper reaches of the Ket valley, presumably through demand from both Whithorn and neighbouring proprietors and farm tenants: see S Ramsay, J Miller, and R Housely, nd, Whithorn Environs: Palaeoenvironmental Investigation of Rispain Mire (First draft. Dept of Archaeology, University of Glasgow).

212 The Murrays of Broughton and Cally, for example, were enclosing their lands in Whithorn parish in the 1730s and renting them out as cattle parks (NAS GD10/1299).

213 T C Smout, *A History of the Scottish People* (London, 1985), 290.

214 I Donnachie and I MacLeod, *Old Galloway* (Newton Abbot, 1974), 12.

215 J Webster, *General View of the Agriculture of Galloway* (Edinburgh, 1794), 2, 4–5.

216 Webster, *Agriculture of Galloway*, 21, 29.

217 *History of the Union of Scotland and England by Sir John Clerk of Penicuik*, trans and ed D Duncan (SHS, 1993), 2–4. For Clerk's involvement in Scottish national financial matters, see GD18/3128, Copy Minute Book of the Commissioners of Parliament for examination of public accounts, 1703–04.

218 Fraser, *Lowland Lore*, 38–9, this was a piece of land whose tenancy had expired. Presumably the same was to be done in other areas as the opportunity arose.

219 *OSA*, 535–6, 539.

220 Webster, *Agriculture of Galloway*, 4–5. Selkirk's property was at St Mary's Isle, south of Kirkcudbright.

221 *OSA*, 561.

222 S Smith, *General View of the Agriculture of Galloway* (London, 1810), 330–1.

223 *OSA*, 563–5.

224 I Donnachie, 'The Economy of Galloway in Historical Perspective', in *The Galloway Project: a Study of the Economy of South West Scotland with Particular Reference to its Tourist Potential* (Scottish Tourist Board, Edinburgh, 1968), 6.10–11.

225 Webster, *Agriculture of Galloway*, 14.

226 Smith, *Agriculture of Galloway*, 329.

227 *OSA*, 571–2.

228 I Donnachie, *The Industrial Archaeology of Galloway* (Newton Abbot, 1971), 68.

229 The tan-pits have been noted by archaeologists, NMRS record NX45NW 5 at NX 4365 5552 (OS visit 17 Sept 1970).

230 Webster, *Agriculture of Galloway*, 14.

231   C Malcolm, *The History of the British Linen Bank* (Edinburgh, 1950), 194.

232   Munn, 1981, 60–1, 174 (it was founded by a Douglas).

233   Smith, *Agriculture of Galloway*, 353

234   S G Checkland, *Scottish Banking: a history 1695–1973* (Glasgow & London, 1975), 174; C Munn, *The Scottish Provincial Banking Companies 1747–1864* (Edinburgh, 1981), 174.

235   NAS E326/4/6 and 8.

236   *The Statistical Account of Scotland 1791–1799: vol. I, General,* eds D J Withrington and I R Grant (Wakefield, 1983), 144–8, 'Population of the Towns of Scotland, containing 300 Souls and upwards'

237   *OSA*, 551 (Whithorn).

238   Brewster, *Wigtown*, 38, 42.

239   Donnachie, *Industrial Archaeology*, 153.

240   Quotation from initial survey, in R H Campbell, *Owners and Occupiers: Changes in Rural Society in South-West Scotland before 1914* (Aberdeen, 1991), 7.

241   W Taylor, *The Military Roads in Scotland* (Newton Abbot, 1976), 100.

242   Taylor, *Military Roads*, 100–1; Webster, *Agriculture of Galloway*, 20; Donnachie, *Industrial Archaeology*, 26. The Road Trustees took over responsibility for the military road in 1807 (Taylor, *Military Roads*, 111).

243   Smith, *Agriculture of Galloway*, 317.

244   *OSA*, 572.

245   C Hill, 'The Maritime Economy of Dumfries and Galloway, 1707–1850', unpublished PhD thesis, University of Strathclyde, 2004, 6.

246   Hill, 'Maritime Economy', 6, 17, 22 (in the 17th century the west coast had come under Ayr, and the head ports on the Solway had been Kirkcudbright and Dumfries), 181, 227.

247   This and the next two paragraphs are based on information derived from NAS CS96/1145–50, documents relating to William Russell and Co, merchants, Wigtown, 1701–04.

248   Possibly the tan-pits identified near the road running up to the town from the old harbour (see p 00).

249   Goods the company handled included wine, brandy, 'hungary water' (like eau de colgone but made with rosemary), spices, dried fruit, nuts, tobacco, alum, gall starch, gunpowder, redwood, yellowwood, brimstone, treacle ('trayakle'), train oil, sweet oil, vinegar, loaf sugar, earthenware, iron cooking pots, brassware, drinking glasses, looking glasses, coal, hemp, twine, writing paper, sealing wax, vegetable seeds, ladies' gloves, playing cards, a glass necklace, and an ivory-handled cane.

250   For more information on this way of storing and repairing ships, see I Friel, *The Good Ship: Ships, Shipbuilding and technology in England 1200–1520* (London, 1995), 52–7.

251   E Graham, *A Maritime History of Scotland* (East Linton, 2002), 124, 128, 238.

252   Pococke, *Tour through Scotland, 1760,* ed D W Kemp (SHS, Edinburgh, 1887), 17.

253   *OSA*, 572.

254   *OSA*, 574.

255 Fraser, *Wigtown and Whithorn*, 34–5, quoting town council minutes of 1774, and the memories of James McWilliam, former excise-officer.

256 Brewster, *Wigtown*, 46, 'It was later used as a lodging house'.

257 Pococke, *Tour*, 18.

258 M'Kerlie, *Lands and their Owners*, 155.

259 *OSA*, 570, though this was not particularly uncommon in small towns.

260 Brewster, *Wigtown*, 42–3.

261 *Wigtown: a Parish History* (1998), 43.

262 *OSA*, 574.

263 Brewster, *Wigtown*, 41; Fraser, *Lowland Lore*, 33–4, in Jun 1712 each fit inhabitant with a horse was ordered by the council to go to the wood of Caldones and 'bring home ane draught of timber for building a schoolhouse', but in May 1713 only half the timber had been fetched.

264 Fraser, *Lowland Lore,* 35, it was decribed as being situated 'without the Friar Vennel'.

265 *OSA*, 571.

266 Smout, *History of the Scottish People*, 439.

267 The grammar school and the parish school were the same, so a separate building was either never built or was found to be uneconomic.

268 Royal Commission on the Ancient and Historical Monuments of Scotland, *Tolbooths and Townhouses: Civic Architecture in Scotland to 1833* (HMSO 1996), 207; Brewster, *Wigtown*, 44, it was said to need gunpowder to demolish it because the mortar was made of powdered cockle shells (this makes sense, according to the Scottish Lime Centre). This pattern of adding to a rebuilt tolbooth during the 18th century to create ballrooms and other facilities, which were relatively soon demolished to make way for a thorough 19th-century rebuild, is seen in many other burghs, such as Cupar (Martin, *Cupar*, 94–8).

269 Fraser, *Wigtown and Whithorn*, 65.

270 Fraser, *Wigtown and Whithorn*, 24; *Wigtownshire Official Guide* (1955), 12, traces of the latter [West Port] existed as recently as twenty years ago'.

271 Fraser, *Wigtown and Whithorn*, 25.

272 J Gifford, *The Buildings of Scotland: Dumfries and Galloway* (London, 1996), 571–2; Brewster, *Wigtown*, 51, it cost £466 17s 10d, £350 from the burgh, and the rest subscribed by local gentry.

273 Fraser, *Wigtown and Whithorn*, 22–3.

274 Brewster, *Wigtown*, 51; Fraser, *Wigtown and Whithorn*, 91–2, while some claim the cross was erected to commemorate the Battle of Waterloo, there is nothing in the town council minutes to suggest this.

275 Brewster, *Wigtown*, 46–7.

276 *Wigtown: a Parish History*, 23.

277 Brewster, *Wigtown*, 50.

278 Brewster, *Wigtown*, 63; *Wigtown's Historic Buildings* (Wigtown and Bladnoch Business Association, nd), 25.

279 Ayrshire Archives B6/39/119, he was to be hanged at Ayr.

280 *NSA*, 5; M Towsey, 'All partners may be enlightened and improved by reading

them': the distribution of Enlightenment books in Scottish subscription library catalogues, 1750–c 1820, *Journal of Scottish Historical Studies* **28**.1 (2008), 28.

281   Brewster, *Wigtown*, 48–9.

282   NAS E326/1/123, 215–16 and 218, *Wigtown's Historic Buildings*, 164, the garden wall is described in the early 19th century as belonging to the park of Nathaniel Agnew.

283   *Wigtown's Historic Buildings*, 39–43.

284   NAS E326/1/216 and 218.

285   *Wigtown's Historic Buildings*, 35–7.

286   NAS E326/3/61 and 63.

287   M'Kerlie, *Lands and their Owners*, 159; Fraser, *Wigtown and Whithorn*, 38, 'Lord Galloway seems to have retained the Provostship of Wigtown during the greater part of the last century'.

288   See for example Martin, *Cupar*, chapter 9.

289   *OSA*, 566, 574 he gives the number of 'Irish, or of Irish parents' as 146, or 11% of the population of the parish.

290   *OSA*, 568, 571.

291   *OSA*, 570.

292   *OSA*, 574

293   NAS E326/15/31.

294   Brewster, *Wigtown*, 42.

295   NAS FS1/27/1.

296   *Poor Law Inquiry Commission for Scotland* (1844), Examinations, Synod of Galloway, Parish of Whithorn, 529, the minister dated the need for regular voluntary contributions from the heritors for the maintenance of the poor as starting from a bad harvest in 1826.

297   *Report upon the boundaries of the several cities burghs and towns of Scotland …* *1832*, 153.

298   *NSA*, 8.

299   M'Kerlie, *Lands and their Owners*, 153, discussing the site of the friary, wrote, 'Previously, in 1818, a portion of the walls was to be seen. At that time tan pits were on the ground'.

300   Hill, 'Maritime Economy', 183, 190, 230, there seems to have been a basin 100ft by 60ft, but in the 1960s this was filled in with material from the demolition of Baldoon airfield buildings; Donnachie, *Industrial Archaeology*, 170; sources differ, but it seems the river changed its course naturally. Graham, 'Old harbours', 66, says the old harbour reverted to farmland. Its site is now under or partly to landward of the railway embankment, which has altered the shoreline and contributed to the build-up of saltmarsh.

301   Brewster, *Wigtown*, 52.

302   *NSA*, 6.

303   A Barnard, *The Whisky Distilleries of the United Kingdom* (1887, repr Newton Abbott, 1969), 342–3.

304   I MacLeod, *Discovering Galloway* (Edinburgh, 1986), 211.

305   *Burgh of Wigtown, Official Guide*, 7.

306 *NSA*, 6.

307 M'Kerlie, *Lands and their Owners*, 160.

308 Birchman, Wigtown Old Kirkyard, no 115

309 Malcolm, *British Linen Bank*, 194, four generations of Blacks served the bank between 1825 and 1933; *NSA*, 7.

310 Brewster, *Wigtown*, 67.

311 F Groome, *Ordnance Gazetteer* (Glasgow, 1894–95).

312 Brewster, *Wigtown*, 53; *NSA*, 6.

313 J Wilson, *Voyage round the Coasts of Scotland* (Edinburgh, 1842), i, 56.

314 NAS BT2/2792.

315 M'Kerlie, *Lands and their Owners,* 160; Hill, 'Maritime Economy', 231.

316 Donnachie, *Industrial Archaeology*, 170; Groome, *Ordnance Gazetteer*.

317 Hill, 'Maritime Economy', 334.

318 Oram *et al*, *Tain* (York, 2009).

319 D L Smith, *The Little Railways of South-West Scotland* (Newton Abbot, 1969), 86–98.

320 Donnachie, *Industrial Archaeology*, 191–4, with map of railway network in Galloway.

321 *Burgh of Wigtown, Official Guide*, 7.

322 Groome, *Ordnance Gazetteer*.

323 *NSA*, 6.

324 Brewster, *Wigtown*, 56–7, quoting a *Gazetteer* published in the first half of the century.

325 MacLeod, *Discovering Galloway*, 210. *Third Statistical Account*, 395, gives the date for this as 1845.

326 Gifford, *Dumfries and Galloway*, 572; Brewster, *Wigtown*, 69–70.

327 Groome, *Ordnance Gazetteer*.

328 Brewster, *Wigtown*, 60–1

329 Gifford, *Dumfries and Galloway*, 571; Brewster, *Wigtown*, 63; *Slater's Directory*, 1889.

330 Brewster, *Wigtown*, 63.

331 RCAHMS, *Tolbooths and Townhouses*, 207; Gifford, *Dumfries and Galloway*, 570–1.

332 *Third Statistical Account*, 391–2. See also Brewster, *Wigtown*, 39; Gifford, *Dumfries and Galloway*, 571, the top was added to match the rest of the building in 1862–63.

333 Groome, *Ordnance Gazetteer*. If this is the case, and the cell looks as if it could be that old, then it must have survived demolition with gunpowder in 1747, and rebuilding in 1747 and 1776, but this is possible if some of the changes involved additions to the original tower rather than complete rebuilding.

334 *NSA*, 8.

335 M'Kerlie, *Lands and their Owners,*159, it remained in use until 1878; Gifford, *Dumfries and Galloway*, 571; *Third Statistical Account*, 392; Brewster, *Wigtown*, 56, there seems to have been an earlier prison, separate from the Town House, looking like a Swiss chalet and located near Lochan Croft; *Wigtown's Historic Buildings*, 15, in 1955 it became a private house.

336 *Third Statistical Account*, 396.

337 M'Kerlie, *Lands and their Owners,* 155.

338 M'Kerlie, *Lands and their Owners,* 159; 300, the 9th Earl of Galloway, although an Episcopalian himself, supported the established church attended by most of his tenants. 'The handsome new parish churches of Minnigaff, Penninghame, Wigton, and Sorbie, remain as records of this, for, as the chief proprietor, he had much to do with their erection.'

339 *Third Statistical Account*, 391.

340 Fraser, *Wigtown and Whithorn*, 234, it was being built by the Relief church but was bought by the Free Church.

341 *Third Statistical Account*, 396.

342 *NSA*, 7.

343 Brewster, *Wigtown*, 58, this school was described in various ways. In Pigot's 1837 *Directory* 'Grammar School and Commercial Academy', in Slater's 1852 *Directory* 'Parochial, Burgh and Grammar School'; Gifford, *Dumfries and Galloway*, 570–1.

344 Brewster, *Wigtown*, 65.

345 Brewster, *Wigtown*, 57; *Wigtown's Historic Buildings*, 20–1, in about 1914 the building became a private house.

346 *Third Statistical Account*, 395.

347 Brewster, *Wigtown*, 52; *Wigtown's Historic Buildings*, 77, 84.

348 Brewster, *Wigtown*, 54; *Wigtown's Historic Buildings*, 86–94.

349 *Wigtown's Historic Buildings*, 95–8.

350 Gifford, *Dumfries and Galloway*, 571. It later became the Wigtown House Hotel.

351 Gifford, *Dumfries and Galloway*, 571–3.

352 Groome, *Ordnance Gazetteer*.

353 Barnard, *Whisky Distilleries*, 1887, 342.

354 *Third Statistical Account*, 393.

355 *NSA*, 5.

356 Immigration was nothing new, but the scale of it changed. *Wigtown parish records. The session book of Wigtown, 1701–1745,* ed H Paton (Edinburgh, 1934), 39, in 1702, for example, the kirk session gave money to '2 distressed women from Ireland', and numerous subsequent entries of charity to named individuals, both men and women, from Ireland, along with shipwrecked sailors, and locals in difficulties.

357 *NSA*, 8.

358 J E Handley, *The Irish in Scotland, 1798–1845* (Cork, 1945), 216; *Poor Law Inquiry,* 534.

359 T M Devine, *The Scottish Nation 1700–2000* (London, 1999), 503–4

360 G Walker, The Protestant Irish in Scotland', in T M Devine ed, *Irish Immigrants and Scottish Society in the Nineteenth and Twentieth Centuries* (Edinburgh, 1991), 48–50; *Report from Select Committee on Orange Institutions in Great Britain and the Colonies* (1835), Report, 24, appendix 19, 143.

361 Campbell, *Owners and Occupiers*, 8.

362 Campbell, *Owners and Occupiers*, 36. Those who could afford it chose to emigrate to America.

363 *Third Statistical Account*, 394.

364 *NSA*, 8.

365 NAS FS1/27/1.

366 Brewster, *Wigtown*, 53.

367 *Third Statistical Account*, 396–7.

368 Fraser, *Wigtown and Whithorn*, 240.

369 Brewster, *Wigtown*, 63.

370 Fraser, *Wigtown and Whithorn*, 240.

371 *Third Statistical Account*, 390.

372 MacLeod, *Discovering Galloway*, 212.

373 *Wigtown: a Parish History*, 36, 135, one page says Kirkland Terrace, the other Kirkland Crescent.

374 *Third Statistical Account*, 389.

375 *Third Statistical Account*, 398.

376 *Third Statistical Account*, 353–4.

377 *Burgh of Wigtown, Official Guide*, 5.

378 *Third Statistical Account*, 394, 398.

379 *Third Statistical Account*, 355–6; *Wigtown's Historic Buildings*, 31–2.

380 *Third Statistical Account*, 391.

381 *Third Statistical Account*, 391, 396.

382 *Third Statistical Account*, 376, 395.

383 *Wigtown: a Parish History*, 26.

384 *Wigtown's Historic Buildings*, 19.

385 *Third Statistical Account*, 372, 394.

386 *Third Statistical Account*, 397–8.

387 *Third Statistical Account*, 392.

388 *Wigtown, a Parish History*, 26.

389 *Third Statistical Account*, 392.

390 *Third Statistical Account*, 393.

391 *Third Statistical Account*, 385.

392 *Wigtown: a Parish History*, 104–5.

4 The potential of Wigtown

Wigtown's most striking characteristic is its disproportionately large, triangular central space (**maps 3 & 6**). It perhaps seems larger because the rest of the town is so small, and the houses on North and South Main Street are mostly too low to give it the sort of sense of enclosure one finds in other burghs. This was the town's 'outdoor room' or principal place of business, its traditional use as a market place signified by the survival of two market crosses. This space was not defined by topography nor by any natural defence, being situated halfway down a south-facing slope. The explanation for the alignment of the north side must be that it sits on the long-established track along which the burgh was laid out.

When the lands of the sheriffdom of Wigtown became an earldom in 1341, Wigtown ceased to be a royal burgh, becoming instead the property of the earl.[1] Strong lordship in this notoriously turbulent zone meant that physical control of Wigtown was important, and in the fifteenth century the Douglases apparently expressed that in the form of a tower – the new fashionable symbol of seigneurial power – within the burgh, as they also did at Galashiels.[2] That was probably all in terms of defensiveness. Typical of almost all Scots burghs, there is no evidence that Wigtown was ever militarily walled, and the fact that it had only two gates, though there were other minor routes in and out of the town, suggests that the East and West Ports represented only control and customs points.

Wigtown suffered no particular loss at the Reformation which affected the burgh's fabric (unlike Whithorn), and the town appears to have remained prosperous until the mid-seventeenth century, after which it seems to have declined. In 1701 the council appealed to the Convention of Royal Burghs for financial aid:

> As to the fabrick of the burgh, that it is visible to any sight that the most half thereof is lying in ane ruined heap altogether fallen to the ground, and a considerable part of the houses standing not possest, and many that are possest are by poor people'.[3]

Four years later it appealed again, claiming that Wigtown had become 'one of the most mean [burghs] in the west', partly as the result of the loss of her principal ship off the coast of Holland.[4] The extent of the deterioration of the fabric during the late seventeenth century is unclear, but a variety of sources point to significant contraction and partial dereliction. It is at least possible that the town lost a body of buildings at its centre. Larger houses were almost certainly cut down and sometimes subdivided, in a manner very similar to nearby Whithorn.[5] Recovery was to be some decades in coming.

All of Wigtown's principal monuments – castle, parish church, harbour and friary – lay on or near the burgh's eastern boundary. Wigtown Castle had been the symbolic centre of crown authority in the sheriffdom. However, its location on the low ground to the south-east implies that it had little or no effect on the layout and growth of the burgh, its purpose being to control the harbour and river-mouth. After a brief occupation by an English garrison during the early years of the Wars of Independence, the castle vanished from history and regional power was vested in the burgh up the hill.

Most descriptions of central Wigtown refer to Main Street as a parallelogram or a square. It is neither. It is triangular in form, broad to the north-east and narrow to the south-west. South Main Street, on the downhill side of this seemingly disproportionately large central space, lies at a completely different angle to North Main Street. A central area sloping and triangular like this is not a typical Scottish market place, but is almost paralleled by that at Dumfries, which is also triangular but slopes downhill from the broad to narrow end rather than across its central axis as at Wigtown. The elite end of the burgh – with tolbooth, kirk, friary, harbour and aristocratic town houses – lay on the broad, lower east side. The service end of the town lay at the upper, narrow end, around the West Port – the inns just within it and stables and workshops and an artisan community initially known as the Town Head (later High Street) just without. The port stood just to the east of where High Vennel debouched from the north into the junction of the routes west to Portpatrick or Stranraer and south to Whithorn. This placing of the street junction outside the area enclosed by the town gates suggests that the West Port was, unusually, enclosing the market place rather than the whole town.[6]

The alignment of North Main Street, which may legitimately be identified with the 'Hie Gait',[7] was clearly governed by the ancient route to the south and west from the Cree ford. Following the pattern of burghs such as Dundee, Montrose or Dumfries, one would have expected the south side of the burgh's market place to be approximately parallel to it; South Main Street is not. While its alignment may have been governed by a route from the burgh to the castle or more likely the friary, it is perhaps possible that the void now at the centre was not originally entirely vacant. There may once have been, or were intended to have been, buildings on this strip of land comparable to the Luckenbooths in Edinburgh or Dundee, the Raws of Montrose or a similar block in Hawick. Buildings on this central site might indeed have been those that had fallen into the 'ruined heap' which the Council lamented in 1701, and were then removed. This hypothesis can only be tested by archaeological or geophysical investigation, but watching briefs in this area in the past have not identified any evidence for significant historic archaeological deposits.

This apparently over-scaled market place has sometimes been explained by the burgh having been originally laid out on too ambitious a scale, and subsequently failing to realise its potential. The sense of disproportionate

FIGURE 25
Cottages in Low Vennel,
before and after restoration
through the Wigtown
Townscape Heritage
Initiative (Mark Watson)

size, however, may be a matter of perception arising from the comparative low-rise character of the enclosing buildings, gaps created in both North and South Main Street for either new road access points or later nineteenth- and twentieth-century construction, and the absence of any substantial structures in its centre. Comparisons with the plans of Dumfries, Haddington, Crail or Elgin, for example, emphasise that the original market areas in these burghs were also, to modern eyes, quite disproportionate to the size of the communities which they then served.

An alternative explanation for the size, slope and enclosed nature of Main Street may lie in the importance of the cattle trade. Closed off by the ports at each end, the square might have served as a holding area for cattle, an arrangement not dissimilar to some northern English communities.[8] Travellers approaching from the north could either enter the market place via Low Vennel (**fig 25**), or use High Vennel to avoid the enclosed central area and continue their journey south or west. Yet although the downslope draining of effluent from beasts may possibly explain why the south, lower side of Main Street seems to have been less popular than the upslope side, that is contradicted by the clear documentary evidence of substantial and high-status ancient structures at the lower level. Moreover, there are no other examples of Scots burghs being laid out *a priori* to form a cattle enclosure. In the absence of firm evidence this has to remain a puzzle.

A visitor entering Wigtown from the Cree ford would have first seen the parish church standing out eastward on its bluff, signalling the town's location. On clambering up the hill, he would have come to the East Port. Once within the gate, he would have found himself within a wide rectangular area (now Bank Street) extending as far west as Low Vennel (which was the principal entrance from the north). This space, apparently later called the Little Square, was dominated by the tolbooth.[9] Here, possibly, lay the market place of old Wigtown, and that might explain its unnaturally wide scale. It was nonetheless much more enclosed and weather-protected than the windswept expanse of Main Street further west; always assuming that, if it was to act effectively as Wigtown's market place, some protection was given to Little Square on its west side against the blast of the prevailing winds blowing up from the south-west.

It is likely that justice was originally dispensed from the Douglases' tower, which is first mentioned in 1451 but which may have been built in the fourteenth century; it is possible that the tower mutated into a tolbooth, the first record of which is in 1587.[10] There is only one other similar known case of a high-status residence being later converted into a tolbooth – at Maybole in South Ayrshire, where the town house of the Kennedys of Blairquhan was bought by the town in 1674 for use as a council meeting-place and tolbooth.[11] Blairquhan's house, however, was not the symbolic seat of a former overlord of the burgh, but simply a large building acquired by Maybole's council, so the parallel is not exact. Symson described the tolbooth as 'standing neer the middle of the town',[12] which may confirm the extent to which elite Wigtown was inclined to the east. Moreover, the primacy of Little Square was emphasised by the fact that, rather than facing westwards over the void of Main Street (if it was a void), the tolbooth tower appears to have faced northwards across Little Square just to the east of the point where Low Vennel entered from the north (site of present County Buildings) (**map 6b**).

The replacement of the tolbooth by a new town house, with a ground-floor piazza or arcade, designed by the architect John Douglas and built by the mason bailie Samuel Kennan, in 1747–49 implies a new-found urban confidence. Unfortunately, this town house was already 'ruinous and decayed' barely 30 years later, and was rebuilt in 1776 with a tall spire (see **fig 15**). When Bishop Pococke had visited in 1760, he had been mildly impressed, for the burgh was beginning to enjoy the generally increasing urban prosperity of the eighteenth and early nineteenth century. To judge by those paying the Window Tax, there were a reasonable number of large houses occupied by a mix of local lairds, professionals and merchants, and there was the beginning of some sporadic suburban villa planning, though construction mostly took place in the first decades of the nineteenth century.

By the yardstick of early nineteenth-century urban Scotland, Wigtown presented a 'very humble, unpretentious, and untidy' appearance, with many single-storeyed thatched cottages.[13] The centre of Main Street was rough grass interspersed with middens and peat stacks. In 1809, the burgh embarked upon a major urban improvement (**map 8**) in transforming the centre into grass terraces 'rising above one another as on the section of a galleried pyramid [where the burghers] may look down on the sport of the bowl-players below'.[14] Surrounded by 'umbrageous gravel walks', and planted

MAP 8
An assessment of the phases
of development of the town

along the side with shrubs, evergreens and forest trees, 'so fine and judicious a burghal ornament as this enclosure with its contents, is quite unique of its kind, indicates much good taste, and ought to provoke imitation'.[15] By 1825, Main Street could be adduced smart: 'the centre laid out in walks and a bowling green, forming an agreeable promenade for the inhabitants'.[16]

Substantial villas now dotted the hinterland, mainly to the south and west. Wigtown had refashioned itself, and its few visitors were suitably impressed. The burgh's status as a gentry town was reflected in the remodelling of many of the houses facing Main Street with smart classical porches, new façades and other contemporary signs of elegance. By 1842 the number of neat, new houses entirely redeemed the burgh from 'the careworn and tawdry aspect which so generally belongs to old Scottish towns of its class'.[17] It was praised for its cleanness, a neatness, and a general taste rarely, if at all, found in towns of its size.

In 1862–63 Wigtown's third tolbooth was finally replaced by a new County Buildings and Town Hall. Designed by Brown and Wardrop in resplendent red and yellow Cumbrian sandstone, its spurious medievalism was intended to add dignity to the town and won the approval of John Ruskin, who occasionally visited friends in the town (**figs 18 & 19**).[18] The earlier tower was incorporated in the centre of the north side and encased in the new armour. Ruskin would, presumably, also have approved of the diminutive cruciform brick-built gothic Roman Catholic Church of the Sacred Heart on South Main Street. Erected in 1879, and seating 250, it was the first Roman Catholic church in the Machars, built to cater for Irish immigrants. As with the parish church, the architect, J Garden Brown, was again selected from London and the design was similarly short on local empathy.

The railway line to Wigtown was opened in 1875, but far from bringing prosperity, it contributed to the decline of the harbour and eventually of the population of the town.[19] Its physical impact on the burgh – beyond the delightful cottage-like Station House, built of yellow greywacke and retaining its clock[20] – appears to have been minimal save that subsequent urban expansion tended to gravitate towards the south side of the town.

Character analysis (map 9)

The East End

This part of Wigtown is characterised by loss. The Little Square, presumably blocked to the east by the East Port, is now Bank Street – a Victorian name for an over-wide space. Lacking any sense of enclosure, this part of town has become denatured, its significance diminished by the widening of Low Vennel. The sole surviving relics of its early importance are the much-altered tolbooth tower itself, and Bank House in its walled garden (**figs 23 & 24**). Although mid-Victorian in its materials, this house sits upon cellars untypical for an urban villa of that date. In the early seventeenth century, this land may have been in the hands of Alexander Agnew of Dalreagle since the garden wall, which effectively forms the eastern boundary of Wigtown (a hospital proposed for the field beyond was never built), was described as belonging to the park of his descendant Nathaniel Agnew of Ochiltree.[21] It is reasonable to suppose that this house occupies the site and possibly cellars of the Agnew house, and that the extraordinarily fine late seventeenth- or early eighteenth-century walled garden with its two-storeyed corner summer/apple houses were built by them (**fig 23**).[22] They might date from the period when the architectural patron Sir John Clerk of Penicuik was MP for the burgh.[23]

Many of the houses in this area are mid-Victorian in their current form; No 11 is dated 1840 and No 12, Mora, is faced with late nineteenth-century granite. The remainder are built of greywacke with dark-red sandstone quoins as in Whithorn, and the roofing is frequently in the English manner,

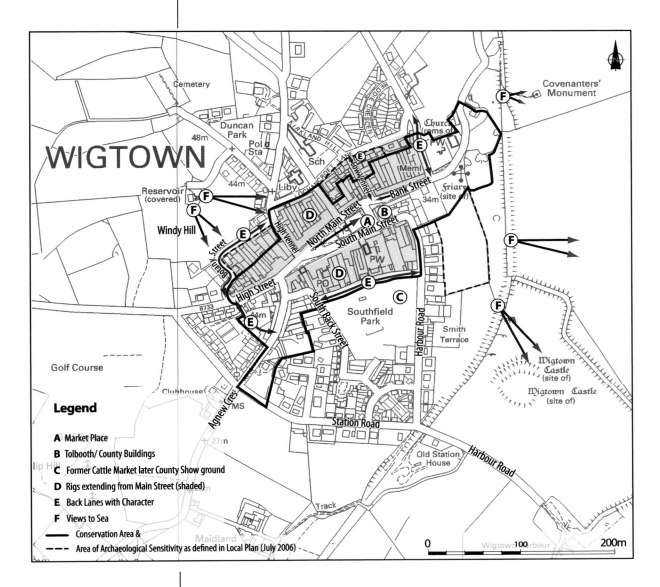

again like Whithorn. Some have an extra, flat-headed doorway which is, in fact a pend leading through to the rear of the property.

Most traffic between the new harbour and the burgh seems to have been directed to the west end of Main Street, and thus would have travelled along the south side of the burgh and up Agnew Crescent. That might explain the indifferent fate of Harbour Road, laid out in 1817 but not formally feued in the manner of Agnew Crescent. It never became fully urbanised, since the town spilled downhill towards the new harbour only sporadically. Harbour Road became, instead, the location of stables, the Free Church and the Free Church school in 1844, on superb sites overlooking the sea. The latter, now converted into the house Dunmore (9 Harbour Road), is a graceful, large-windowed single-storey red stone school with hoodmoulds above the windows.

The only civic building in this new road was the prison, designed by Thomas Brown junior. Built of red and grey stone in 1846–48, like a cross between an Elizabethan manor and a factory with hoodmoulds above the windows, the prison became the first public building to be seen by passengers arriving by sea or alighting at the railway station (**fig 20**). Its notable finials and chimneys sit within a nice defensively walled enclosure.[24] In 1881 it was converted for use as a police station, and later into flats.[25]

The kirk's impressive scale was evidence of the burgh's medieval success. It was enlarged with chapels in the sixteenth century, and repaired in the seventeenth and eighteenth centuries. However, the decline of the burgh during the later seventeenth century and its slow recovery is perhaps symbolised by the fact that it was 1851 before the old church was finally replaced by a much larger granite god-box with 660 sittings, designed by the London architect, Henry Roberts (**fig 18**). The corner buttresses, chamfered plinth, string-course and blocked windows of the medieval church are still visible at the east gable of the old church. A gothic window and a later mullioned one with its glazing check survive in the remains of the Vans (Vaus) burial aisle, which was added to the south side of the nave in the later medieval period. The ruins of the church were cleared of ivy and the masonry consolidated in 2010, allowing appreciation of the building once again (see **fig 5**). The rich and atmospheric sloping graveyard has a fine selection of gravestones (**fig 10**).

North Main Street

While the sweep of buildings along North Main Street appears to be later eighteenth or early nineteenth century, when Wigtown put on a smart new face,[26] there is some evidence that a number of these properties contain older structures within, and that their current scale indicates higher buildings cut down later. 'Pretty good houses three storey high toward the street' predominated on the north side in the later seventeenth century,[27] and these were likely to be the town houses of regional landowners such as the Agnews, Carlisles of Torthorwald, Dunbars of Baldoon, McGarvies, Makcristens, Murrays of Broughton, and Vaus of Barnbarroch. Judging from Low Vennel's other name – 'Hannay's Vennel'[28] – it was probably on the corner of Little Square and Low Vennel that William Ahannay was given licence in 1549 to build his great stone house.

More of these houses survive within later structures than is currently acknowledged. The now-demolished Red Lion Inn (formerly the town house of the Dunbars of Baldoon) had wall-thicknesses implying a date of the late fifteenth or early sixteenth century, as recorded during alteration in 1936 (see **fig 14**).[29] Its plan was comparable to that surviving in No 17 North Main Street in

FIGURE 26
Doric-columned porch at pend entrance of No 17 North Main Street (Richard Oram)

that the ground floor comprised two chambers facing the street, which may originally have been arcaded, entirely separate from the two-storeyed house above. The latter was entered down a close and up a turnpike stair at the rear,[30] and comprised two chambers per floor facing the street, and a single one projecting north. Although No 17 presents the smart classical façade added by the provost George McHaffie *c* 1830,[31] this complex has much more significance than the façade alone. One of the tallest buildings in North Main Street, the house was originally entered from the side, the pend leading to it adorned with a fine Doric-columned porch (**fig 26**). Its upper walls have clearly been rebuilt, there are blocked openings, and on one of its skews there is a carved face. The interior largely reflects the late classical sophistication of McHaffie – a fine staircase, nice rooms and good plasterwork – but its structure is likely to incorporate material from centuries earlier.

No 11 North Main Street contains an enormous sixteenth- or seventeeth-century kitchen fireplace in a rear extension, almost certainly a relic of a much larger mansion destroyed by the insertion of New Road. Its eastern neighbour could be of comparable age. The 1960s' flats in the stretch of North Main Street between New Road and Low Vennel with the datestone 'MK 1819' were built on the site of the Red Lion Inn. Other inherited relics include buildings which have battered rather than vertical walls, and a number are entered on one side rather than through the centre as one would expect after the mid-eighteenth century. Materials are various: No 19 North Main Street is constructed of granite with cherry cocking. The post office, of greywacke and sandstone in Whithorn Style, has a flat above, and its original door is blocked.

South Main Street

Architecturally, South Main Street is similar to North Main Street comprising mainly two- to three-storeyed, apparently early nineteenth-century houses, many concealing a comparable variety of older fabric. Glaisnock has differences of wall-thickness and changes of floor-level indicative of alterations to an earlier structure. From a datestone, there is evidence of much alteration to No 14 South Main Street in 1730.[32] It also reveals a different pattern of entrance and

FIGURE 28
(above) a, No 29 South Main Street, formerly the
Clydesdale Bank, with b, detail of ironwork (Paula Martin
and Richard Oram)

FIGURE 29
(a–c, at right) Applegarth, a house which does not know
which way to face, and stands on a strangely shaped plot,
both hinting at an interesting history. West and south fronts
(a), south front (b) and east front (c)
(Colin Martin and Richard Oram)

evolution through its pend. No 7/8 was the house of the Collector of Customs,
before the City of Glasgow Bank built its premises in its front garden. From
its rear, however, it becomes evident that the principal floor was the first floor,
implying that the ground floor was the customary cellars and kitchens of an
older town house (**fig 27**). It has a rather fine arched early nineteenth-century
buffet recess within. No 23 has a pedimented, curiously off-centre Doric porch,
while No 29, with its tripartite windows of *c* 1840, and ornate cresting, is sitting

FIGURE 30
Fairholme, perhaps forced
to reorientate when it was
blocked by County Buildings,
although the steps to its door
are shown on the 1848 Town
Plan (1:1056) (Colin Martin)

upon much older cellars (**fig 28**). Avongail has an unusually tall, square rear stair-tower and steep roof which would be worthy of investigation.

Wigtown is fortunate in having such complete southern 'back dykes' running between the rear of each rig and the South Field boundary wall, with a very fine sense of enclosure. Unfortunately, the condition of many of the plots is indifferent: there are crumbling rear rigs, car parking, some dereliction, and some unsympathetic new construction. Its eastern end meets Harbour Road just south of Applegarth (previously Rochdale) (**fig 29**). The latter, said to have been built as a manse in 1814, looks as though it has changed its alignment, and probably incorporates an older building with a basement.[33] Just to the west, and attached to the Town House, Fairholme presents a later eighteenth-century appearance (**fig 30**), but its lack of symmetry and thick walls imply that it may contain an earlier building, possibly of the sixteenth century, re-oriented from west to south.

FIGURE 31
Nos 28–32 High Street, south
side, forestairs (Paula Martin)

FIGURE 32
The top of Agnew Crescent,
with a typical angled corner
on the right-hand building
(Colin Martin)

West and South

Towards the end of the eighteenth century, houses in the craft suburb of Town Head (later High Street or the 'high end of town') were rebuilt further back from the road edge making it marginally wider for traffic to Stranraer.[34] Many of the inns lay on South Main Street just inside the West Port, their stables accessible from the back without entering the market place. A new market cross was constructed at the west end, just inside the West Port, in 1816[35] and a weighbeam installed, indicating the extent to which the economy of the town was shifting westwards. High Street houses were generally smaller and less pretentious than those in Main Street – the simple No 3 High Street, for example, probably divided into three separate apartments – and bore all the characteristics of small dwellings for artisans and labourers. The nearer they were to the road junction the grander they became. Whereas No 32 High Street is characterised by a forestair, as is the typically two-storeyed No 30, and built of granite with cherry cocking (**fig 31**), houses further east were considerably grander. No 1/1a High Street, *c* 1820, later the Edinburgh and Glasgow Bank, built of ashlar sandstone rare in Wigtown, was adorned with good plasterwork and staircase. With its quoins and cornice, No 3 High Street likewise exuded prosperity.

The catalyst behind west-end prosperity may have been the formalisation of the ancient road south to Whithorn by the creation of the curving Agnew Crescent. 'Bending round in the form of a segment of a circle' to lessen the effect of the slope, with a chamfered-cornered building on its eastern corner (**fig 32**), it was feued with sturdy houses as part of a 'new town' development in the early nineteenth century. There had been some houses on it by the later eighteenth century, possibly replaced in the later feuing. The details of the formal houses and cottages of Agnew Crescent are late classical: No 9 has lozenge skewputts, No 11 Doric pilasters, and Nos 22–28 on the east side are all of a piece, with their double doors, quoins and cornices. Acre Place, 1827,[36] is substantial and handsome with a rectangular fanlight and has what appears to be the remains of a lodge attached to its southern gable. It was on this side of Wigtown that detached villas began to appear: Orchardton House built 1820–27 by one of the Maclellan brothers who had set up the Bladnoch distillery; Beechwood (1820), with its orchard, stables, and odd site profile, secluded in its trees at the foot of the Crescent; Barbadoes Villa (1833) (see **fig 22**); and Woodside (1836).[37]

Kilquhirn Road, a broad vennel at the high end of town where the Town Head came to an end, is a fine, sloping passage which joins the High Street

FIGURE 33
Kilquhirn Road/Lane,
looking south (Richard
Oram)

FIGURE 34
Part of the former brewery
buildings, roofed with large
slates (Richard Oram)

to Agnew Crescent, past the evidently historic landscape of Kilquhirn Cottage (**fig 33**). Appropriate to the service end of town, Wigtown's brewery lay uphill behind High Street at the end of the long rigs in Botany (effectively the back dykes of this part of town). It survives in part though much altered for later industrial or agricultural uses (**fig 34**). The original sense of enclosure of the rigs has been eroded, and Botany is now predominantly late twentieth century. 'Sunny Braes', a cottage dated 1874, facing west on the bluff, has curious granite lintels and a cast-iron cornice / gutter; it gives the appearance of the reworking of an older building.

North of the centre

In the 1840s, the two streets – presumably Low and High Vennels – 'each about 130 yards long' that led north off Main Street, and three shorter ones, probably closes, still remained 'not fully edificed'.[38] The back dykes of North Main Street, however, were formalised as Lochancroft Lane and built up with cottages. That edge is still apparent, although the scale has been eroded by later developments to the north, and many of the houses have been greatly altered. Frequently interesting details indicate nineteenth-century pride: for example, the bargeboarding and finials of Fairview and a railway carriage in the substantial garden of Lochancroft House.

Land north of Lochancroft was used for the public buildings of the town: a new parish / burgh school built in 1845, the Gas Works, and a Charity School added by 1867.[39] After the driving through of New Road, All Souls Roman Catholic school was built there. In 1910, the burgh school was expanded and rebuilt.[40] Absence of an overall plan resulted in northern Wigtown lacking any sense of urban enclosure: large institutions on large plots simply replaced the large gardens of earlier houses. Some isolated but substantial Victorian cottages were constructed when Duncan Road was opened, such as the yellow Duncan Cottage.

Bladnoch

The village became the centre of thriving industry, the distillery being joined by a Potato and Farina Mill, a coach-builder, an iron foundry, shops and workshops.[41] The village now consists principally of ribbon development on one side of the road facing the river, with gardens on the river side, presenting a generally early nineteenth-century appearance. Most are cottages, but Rowallan has roll mouldings around windows and doors implying either greater pretension or reuse of masonry from elsewhere. No 33 Bladnoch stands out as the most sophisticated house in the row; perhaps it was the distillery manager's house. Built of fine sandstone, it has a channelled rusticated ground floor, its door enhanced by Doric pilasters and fanlight, and fashionable octagonal chimneys. In the land behind, beside the garage, there is an intriguing twentieth-century industrial building with large metal windows.

Twentieth-century change

The principal additions to Wigtown during the twentieth century have been houses – private houses and social houses mostly added around the perimeter, although there have been some regrettable additions to Main Street. Some of the early 1920s–1930s Addison Act council houses were particularly fine. Semi-detached cottages at the foot of Agnew Crescent have delicate twin gables, lozenge-pattern decoration and alternating door frames. These carry on round the corner, becoming even more distinctive in Lightlands Avenue. Benvoir, a strikingly intrusive red-brick half-timbered Tudor design of 1930 by James Taylor, was built as a doctor's house and surgery on the edge of the golf course.[42]

Some time in the later 1940s, airfield buildings (probably from Baldoon) were dismantled and brought to Wigtown for the Dairy, being re-erected across the road from the school. Since the war, there has been significant construction of social housing in the corner bounded by Station and Harbour Roads, and some private developments below the South Field in Beddie Crescent. More intrusive is the housing construction on the north-east of the town toward Lovers' Walk which both breaks into the skyline of the town when seen from the harbour and blocks views of the sea from houses further inland. Whereas the former were mostly harled, albeit grey cement-harled, the latter are mostly constructed of brick, as though to emphasise their lack of empathy with burgh character. The other principal changes in the twentieth century relate either to the arrival of small-scale industrial concerns, often housed in brick and corrugated iron sheds, petrol stations and motor mechanics' workshops, or to private developments such as garages built by the new car-owning public on the backlands of their properties.

The construction of social housing around the town's perimeter, interspersed with the occasional villa and later housing estate, had the effect of progressively softening one of the burgh's great assets: namely its hard edge with its splendid surrounding countryside. At the same time, the town centre was allowed to decay, a decline exacerbated, perhaps, by the closure of the railway. By the 1990s, decay had become palpable, but the establishment of Wigtown as Scotland's Book Town has stimulated the conversion of a number of properties to bookshops or cafés, and the burgh evinces a revived level of care and maintenance. Main Street remains a space of wide roads, a bowling green, and later market cross, and it comes to life during the annual Book Festival with its attendant farmers' market. If the burgh still has the sense of being a backwater, it now also makes a worthy destination.

Conservation: the Townscape Heritage Initiative

Wigtown Conservation Area was designated in 1977, and its boundary amended in 1999.

The Townscape Heritage Initiative (THI) was launched by the Heritage Lottery Fund in 1998 as a means of promoting regeneration and good management of conservation areas that are experiencing social or economic difficulties. Wigtown was one of the first to win an award and £1.6 million was invested into the Conservation Area by a range of public bodies, more than matched by private investment (**fig 35**). The project was managed for Dumfries and Galloway Council by Solway Heritage. This has produced a useful level of documentation against which to measure change: a public realm survey, a condition survey and a character appraisal produced in 1999–2000. Wigtown was one of the three THIs in Scotland subject to evaluation for the Heritage Lottery Fund by Oxford Brookes University.

The evaluation found, five years on, the community to be more tight-knit and more sustainable. The townscape and conservation

FIGURE 35
No 11 North Main Street (left, in 1980s, right 2007). The substantial Ionic doorpiece belongs to a house that had been very run down but now shows how far Wigtown has come thanks to investment by private owners and by the Wigtown Townscape Heritage Initiative

quality had improved, vacancy rates had dramatically fallen, retail demand and property values had risen and the image as Book Town was well established. Repair and use of the County Buildings was seen as critical to achieving this: the building reopened in 2003 and was the winner in its category of a Scottish Enterprise 'Dynamic Place Award' in 2004.[43]

Issues for the future

The character of central Wigtown still has some damaging gaps in its fabric – particularly in its enclosing street walls. In an ideal world the authors would suggest returning a sense of the medieval enclosure of Little Square to Bank

MAP 10
Listed buildings and known archaeological sites
(see Appendix 1 for gazetteer)

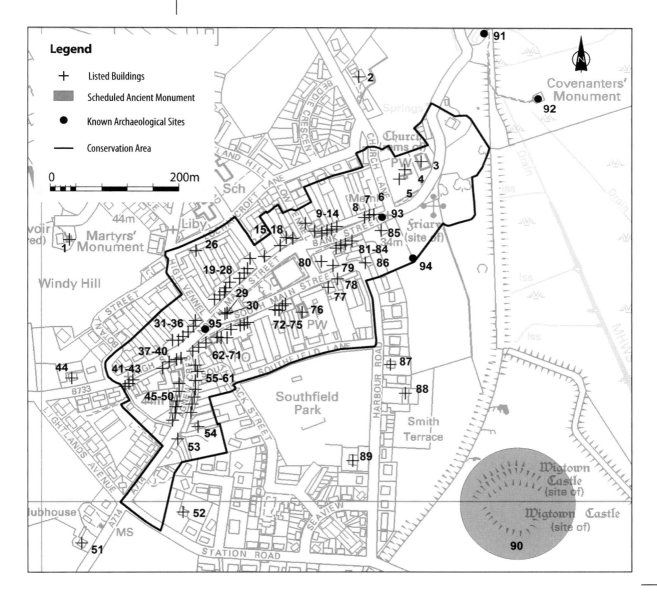

Street and the area around the former East Port, or reintroducing some form of partial closure of Main Street on the line of the West Port, but this is probably unrealistic. However, the long rigs lining the south and north-east of the centre represent a valuable component of the burgh's character, to be cherished and protected from further piecemeal erosion. Gaps in other streets need to be filled, and High Vennel – once a thoroughfare of importance – presents an opportunity for development as it is now much diminished, with some of its buildings demolished.

The Local Plan for Wigtown identifies an Area of Archaeological Sensitivity that corresponds with that of the Conservation Area (**map 10**). The Council's Archaeologist will advise on the level of investigation that may be needed depending on the type of work envisaged.

Crucial to understanding Wigtown's evolution is resolving the origins of the town's market place and the nature and purposes of Main Street and the medieval Little Square (now Bank Street). Three other areas also merit particular attention:

- First, the extent of the survival of older fabric concealed within what, to the outside, appear to be early nineteenth-century houses facing both sides of Main Street should be surveyed. A number of buildings have been highlighted in this report as likely to incorporate much older fabric and they are unlikely to be the only ones.
- Secondly, the location of the friary should be further investigated.
- Finally, Bank House with its exceptional garden deserves study, and its garden pavilions merit restoration.

These matters, when put together, highlight a conclusion that the better understanding of Wigtown during its sixteenth- and early seventeenth-century heyday, and the better presentation of fabric surviving from that period, could contribute significantly to the burgh's already remarkable regeneration as a visitor destination.

Notes

1 *RRS*, **vi**, no 39.
2 *RMS*, **ii**, no 503; M Rorke, D Gallagher, C McKean, E P Dennison and G Ewart, *Historic Galashiels* (CBA, York, 2011).
3 Edinburgh City Archives, Convention of Royal Burghs papers, SL 30/223, Report of the State and Conditione of the Burgh of Wigtoune, 10.6.1701.
4 Edinburgh City Archives, CRB papers, SL 30/223 Supplication of the Burgh of Wigtoun.
5 See Oram *et al*, *Whithorn*.
6 It is possible that the original burgh boundary is defined by the ports, and that the west end was a later addition, but no evidence has been found to suggest this.
7 *RSS*, **iv**, no 502.

8 C H Dick, *Highways and Byways in Galloway and Carrick* (Edinburgh, 1924), 186–7; Brooke, 'Wigtown', 54.

9 Truckell, 'Wigtown Burgh Court Book', 68, refers to the 'greit skayre', from which later commentators identified the smaller area in front of the north side of the town hall as the 'little square'. The name does not seem to have any pre-18th-century authority to support it, but is adopted here as a definition for the broad upper section of Bank Street. As we do not know which side of Low Vennel was sacrificed to widen it, or whether both sides were, its precise alignment cannot be confirmed. Nor do we know exactly where the East Port stood. Indeed we do not know where the earliest tolbooth stood. If it were on an island site, it is possible that the 'little square' was the part of the market place to its east.

10 *RMS*, **ii**, no 503; Fraser, *Lowland Lore*, 53.

11 E P Dennison, D Gallagher and G Ewart, *Historic Maybole: Archaeology and Development* (CBA, York, 2005), 25–8.

12 Symson, *Large Description*, 36.

13 Pococke, *Tour*, 18.

14 Gifford, *Dumfries and Galloway*, 571–2; Brewster, *Wigtown*, 51.

15 *The Topographical, Statistical and Historical Gazetteer of Scotland* (Glasgow, 1842), 810.

16 *Pigot's Directory*.

17 *Topographical, Statistical and Historical Gazetteer of Scotland*, 810.

18 RCAHMS, *Tolbooths and Townhouses*, 207; Gifford, *Dumfries and Galloway*, 570–1; *Third Statistical Account*, 391 (Ruskin reference).

19 Smith, *Little Railways of South-West Scotland*, 86–98; *Burgh of Wigtown, Official Guide*, 7.

20 NAS RHP 84739, 84751 and 84757.

21 *Wigtown's Historic Buildings*, 164.

22 Gifford, *Dumfries and Galloway*, 571.

23 Groome, *Ordnance Gazetteer*; Gifford, *Dumfries and Galloway*, 569–70 puts the date in the 1730s but offers no evidence.

24 NAS RHP 21824-21848.

25 M'Kerlie, *Lands and their Owners*, 159, it remained in use until 1878; Gifford, *Dumfries and Galloway*, 571; *Third Statistical Account*, 392; Brewster, *Wigtown*, 56.

26 Gifford, *Dumfries and Galloway*, 571–3.

27 Symson in MacFarlane, *Geographical Collections*, 74

28 Fraser, *Lowland Lore*, 36.

29 NAS RHP 30086, architectural plan, elevation and detail of Old Red Lion Inn, Wigtown.

30 Later replaced by a scale and platt stair.

31 *Wigtown's Historic Buildings*, 121.

32 *Wigtown's Historic Buildings*, 44.

33 Brewster, *Wigtown*, 63.

34 Fraser, *Wigtown and Whithorn*, 25.

35 Brewster, *Wigtown*, 51; Fraser, *Wigtown and Whithorn*, 91–2.

36 *Wigtown's Historic Buildings*, 77, 84.

37 Brewster, *Wigtown*, 50, 52.

38 *Topographical, Statistical and Historical Gazetteer*, 810.

39 Brewster, *Wigtown*, 58, 65.

40 Gifford, *Dumfries and Galloway*, 570–1.

41 Fraser, *Wigtown and Whithorn*, 240.

42 *Wigtown's Historic Buildings*, 99–101, designed by James Taylor of Glasgow, it incorporated the first doctor's surgery, and the first shower to be installed in the town.

43 *Townscape Heritage Initiative Schemes Evaluation, Wigtown* (Townscape Heritage Research Unit, Dept of Planning, Oxford Brookes University, 2007).

Appendix 1: Significant buildings identified during the Survey

No.	Name	NGR	NMRS No.	Statutory Status	Historic Scot Ref
1	Windy Hill Martyrs' Monument and Enclosure	NX 43754 55633	NX45NW 1	B	42442
2	Church Lane, The Laigh House (Former Manse)	NX 43482 55666	NX45NW 105	C	42386
3	Wigtown Parish Church (Church of Scotland) and Churchyard	NX 43577 55531	NX45NW 15.00	B	42441
4	Wigtown Old Parish Church (St Machute's Church)	NX 43552 55518	NX45NW 4	B	42440
5	Wigtown Parish Church (Church of Scotland) and Churchyard	NX 43544 55503	NX45NW 15.01	B	42441
6	24 Bank Street	NX 43505 55447	NX45NW 103	C	42362
7	22 Bank Street	NX 43498 55446	NX45NW 102	C	42361
8	20 Bank Street	NX 43491 55442	NX45NW 101	C	42360
9	10 Bank Street	NX 43449 55428	NX45NW 100	B	42359
10	8 Bank Street	NX 43441 55424	NX45NW 99	C	42358
11	6 Bank Street	NX 43434 55422	NX45NW 47	B	42357
12	4 Bank Street	NX 43426 55418	NX45NW 98	C	42356
13	2 Bank Street	NX 43415 55421	NX45NW 97	C	42355
14	5 Low Vennel, Smithy	NX 43401 55433	NX45NW 34	C	42400
15	3A & 3B North Main Street	NX 43382 55410	NX45NW 110	C	42401
16	4 North Main Street, The Red Lion Inn	NX 43372 55411	NX45NW 66	C	42402
17	5 & 7 North Main Street	NX 43363 55399	NX45NW 111	C	42403
18	11 North Main Street	NX 43339 55382	NX45NW 69	B	42404
19	12 North Main Street	NX 43317 55379	NX45NW 26	C	42405
20	13 North Main Street	NX 43313 55363	NX45NW 114	C	42406
21	14 North Main Street	NX 43308 55356	NX45NW 115	C	42407
22	15 North Main Street	NX 43301 55348	NX45NW 25	C	42408
23	17 North Main Street	NX 43286 55342	NX45NW 117	B	42409
24	18 North Main Street	NX 43280 55333	NX45NW 118	C	42410
25	19 North Main Street	NX 43278 55327	NX45NW 24	C	42411
26	3 Bank Street	NX 43235 55391	NX45NW 92	C	42350
27	20 North Main Street	NX 43271 55322	NX45NW 119	C	42412
28	21 North Main Street, Bank of Scotland	NX 43263 55315	NX45NW 120	C	42413
29	The Square, Old Market Cross	NX 43282 55294	NX45NW 40.00	B	42438
30	The Square, New Market Cross	NX 43279 55292	NX45NW 40.01	B	42437
31	27 North Main Street	NX 43234 55282	NX45NW 122	C	42414
32	28 North Main Street	NX 43231 55273	NX45NW 123	C	42415
33	29 & 30 North Main Street	NX 43223 55264	NX45NW 124	B	42416
34	31 North Main Street	NX 43215 55257	NX45NW 125	C	42417
35	33 North Main Street, The Granite House	NX 43208 55251	NX45NW 127	C	42418
36	34 North Main Street, The Granite House	NX 43199 55251	NX45NW 128	C	42419

No.	Name	NGR	NMRS No.	Statutory Status	Historic Scot Ref
37	2 High Street	NX 43212 55223	NX45NW 20	C	42393
38	4 High Street	NX 53205 55221	NX45NW 70	C	42394
39	6 & 8 High Street	NX 43194 55217	NX45NW 162	C	42395
		NX 43199 55220		C	
40	10 & 12 High Street	NX 43184 55207	NX45NW 163	C	42396
		NX 43189 55214		C	
41	28 High Street	NX 43139 55189	NX45NW 72	C	42397
42	30 High Street	NX 43133 55183	NX45NW 73	C	42398
43	32 High Street	NX 43127 55179	NX45NW 74	C	42399
44	Fountainblue Terrace, Craigmont Guest House	NX 43046 55192	NX45NW 108	C	42388
45	9 Agnew Crescent	NX 43209 55183	NX45NW 79	C	42337
46	11 & 13 Agnew Crescent	NX 43209 55171	NX45NW 80	C	42338
		NX 43207 55164		C	
47	15 Agnew Crescent, Rowan House	NX 43206 55156	NX45NW 81	C	42339
48	17 Agnew Crescent	NX 43204 55147	NX45NW 67.00	C	42340
49	19 Agnew Crescent	NX 43203 55137	NX45NW 82	C	42341
50	21 Agnew Crescent	NX 43199 55126	NX45NW 83	C	42342
51	Woodside with coach house, retaining wall and railings	NX 43061 54934	NX45SW 53	B	42443
52	Dunure House boundary walls, gates and outbuildings	NX 43215 54983	NX45SW 51	B	42387
53	1–4 (inclusive Nos) Acre Place	NX 43207 55097	NX45NW 78	C	42336
		NX 43205 55092		C	
		NX 43201 55086		C	
		NX 43199 55081		C	
54	26 & 28 Agnew Crescent	NX 43238 55116	NX45NW 91	C	42349
55	18 & 20 Agnew Crescent	NX 43227 55138	NX45NW 90	B	42348
56	16 Agnew Crescent	NX 43229 55151	NX45NW 89	C	42347
57	14 Agnew Crescent	NX 43232 55162	NX45NW 88	C	42346
58	10 Agnew Crescent	NX 43234 55174	NX45NW 87	C	42345
59	8 Agnew Crescent	NX 43234 55188	NX45NW 86	C	42344
60	6 Agnew Crescent	NX 43237 55202	NX45NW 85	C	42343
61	4 Agnew Crescent	NX 43234 55212	NX45NW 84	C	43767
62	33 & 34 South Main Street	NX 43230 55234	NX45NW 140	C	42436
63	31 & 32 South Main Street	NX 43239 55240	NX45NW 139	B	42435
64	29 & 30 South Main Street, County Hotel	NX 43250 55247	NX45NW 22	C	42434
65	28 South Main Street, Craiglachie	NX 43267 55256	NX45NW 138	B	42433
66	27 South Main Street, Post Office	NX 43273 55255	NX 4327 5525	C	43768
67	26 South Main Street	NX 43282 55255	NX45NW 23.01	C	42432
68	25 South Main Street	NX 43288 55268	NX45NW 136	C	42431
69	24 South Main Street	NX 43302 55274	NX45NW 135	B	42430
70	23 South Main Street, Galloway Inn	NX 43308 55276	NX45NW 134	B	42429
71	22 South Main Street	NX 43313 55279	NX45NW 141	B	42428
72	18 South Main Street	NX 43355 55299	NX45NW 133	B	42427
73	16 South Main Street, Sunningdale	NX 43361 55298	NX45NW 132	C	42426
74	15 South Main Street	NX 43366 55305	NX45NW 131	C	42425

No.	Name	NGR	NMRS No.	Statutory Status	Historic Scot Ref
75	14 South Main Street	NX 43371 55308	NX45NW 130	C	42424
76	South Main Street, Sacred Heart Roman Catholic Church with gates, gateposts, railings and boundary walls	NX 43396 55295	NX45NW 104	C	42420
77	8 South Main Street, The Old Custom House and Bank with railings	NX 43436 55334	NX45NW 35	B	42423
78	6 South Main Street	NX 43450 55347	NX45NW 129	B	42422
79	4 South Main Street and garden wall	NX 43443 55368	NX45NW 31	B	42421
80	The Square, Town Hall	NX 43425 55374	NX45NW 107	B	42439
81	7 Bank Street	NX 43448 55395	NX45NW 93	C	42351
82	9 Bank Street	NX 43455 55399	NX45NW 94	C	42352
83	11 Bank Street	NX 43462 55401	NX45NW 95	C	42353
84	13 & 15 Bank Street	NX 43472 55406	NX45NW 96	C	42354
85	Bank Street, Bank House garden wall and garden houses	NX 43516 55422	NX45NW 32.00	B	42363
		NX 43535 55440		B	
		NX 43551 55366		B	
		NX 43563 55375		B	
86	Harbour Road, Applegarth	NX 43492 55372	NX45NW 30	C	42389
87	9 Harbour Road, former manse boundary wall and gatepiers	NX 43530 55213	NX45NW 76	B	42392
88	Harbour Road, Dunmore with gates, gatepiers and boundary walls	NX 43553 55168	NX45NW 75	C	42390
89	Harbour Road, Clintz House with boundary walls (former jail and police station)	NX 43539 54869	NX45SW 50	B	42391
90	Wigtown Castle	NX 43723 54995	NX45NW 2	SAM	11055
91	Old Harbour	NX 43666 55734			
92	Covenanters' monument and enclosure	NX 49754 55634	NX45NW 16	B	42442
93	East Port	NX 43525 55448	NX45NW 18		
94	Friary (approximate site of)	NX 43563 55375			
95	West Port	NX 43131 55195	NX45NW 17		

Glossary

ayre	The circuit of justices for criminal cases and of the Chamberlain to review the affairs of royal burghs.
bailie	The top councillors were provost, bailies (usually between two and four), treasurer and Dean of Guild. These 'magistrates' ran the town on a day-to-day basis, called council meetings etc.
barony	The land or lands controlled by a baron.
burgage	A tenure by which lands or tenements in burghs were held of a superior for an annual rent; the tenements held under that tenure.
burgess	Member of the core of craftsmen and merchants within a burgh, who had exclusive privileges within the burgh. Membership could be inherited, acquired by marriage to a burgess's daughter, or purchased.
burgh of regality	Similar to a burgh of barony, but with more royal powers delegated to the baron.
charter	Formal legal document, usually issued by the crown or a superior lord, detailing the properties, rights and obligations of the recipient.
common good	The lands or other sources of income which were held and managed by a burgh on behalf of its inhabitants.
compear	Scots legal term for making a formal recorded appearance at a legal process or assembly
feu	Grant of land rights. In exchange for a fixed sum and a continued fixed annual rent, a tenant bought the right to hold a property in perpetuity, and to bequeath or sell it.
guildry	Merchant guild, entered by family links or purchase, with exclusive rights to trade within the liberties of a burgh.
intromit	Scots legal term for handling or dealing with funds or property, especially those of another person, with or without legal authority to do so.
harling	The traditional coating for rubble stone walls in Scotland, whether high-status or vernacular, both as a protection from the weather, and to create the impression of geometric mass. Formed from a mixture of usually local gravel bound with lime.

infeft	The process by which an individual is given possession of property or rights by a superior lord.
merk	A medieval unit of account equivalent to 13 shillings and 4d or two-thirds of a pound sterling.
midden	Rubbish heap, whether domestic, agricultural or mixed.
patronage	The right of appointment. The right of landowners to appoint ministers of the Church of Scotland had long been contentious, and eventually led to the Disruption in 1843.
provost	The chief magistrate of a burgh.
regality	Lands and associated rights of jurisdiction where the landlord exercised all rights and legal powers usually associated with the crown – except the right to try treason cases – and where authority of royal justiciars and sheriffs did not operate. Abolished in 1747.
royal burgh	A burgh which paid taxes direct to the crown in exchange for the right to self-government, and whose rights included foreign trade.
tenement	Land or real property held of another by any form of tenure; in Scotland a large building let in portions to a number of tenants.
tolbooth	The central administrative building of a burgh, usually combining council and court rooms, weigh house and prison.
vennel	A narrow passage or lane between buildings, usually in a burgh.

Bibliography

Primary sources

Ayrshire Archives B6/39/119

Dublin, City Archives, 1/1, 2m [Dublin Freedom Rolls]

Edinburgh City Archives, Convention of Royal Burghs papers, SL 30/223, Report of the State and Conditione of the Burgh of Wigtoune

NAS BT2/2792

NAS CS96/1145–50

NAS E326/1/123, 215–16 and 218, Window Tax

NAS E326/3/61 and 63, Inhabited House Tax

NAS E326/4/6 and 8, Shop Tax

NAS E326/15/31, Consolidated Taxes

NAS FS1/27/1, Friendly Societies

NAS GD1 Miscellaneous small collections of family, business and other papers

NAS GD10 Papers of the Murray Family of Broughton, Wigtownshire, and Cally, Kirkcudbrightshire 1410–1978

NAS GD18/3128, Copy Minute Book of the Commissioners of Parliament for examination of public accounts, 1703–1704

NAS RHP 30086, 84739, 84751, 84757, 21824–48

NRAS 76/1

NRAS 631 Marquesses of Bute, NRAS 631/4 McDowell of Freugh titles

Maps and plans

Ainslie, J, Map of the County of Wigton, 1782

British Library, Roy map, c 1750

Ordnance Survey, 1:10560, first edition, surveyed 1848, published 1849; second edition 1894; third edition 1907

Report upon the boundaries of the several cities burghs and towns of Scotland ... 1832, map of Parliamentary boundary of Whithorn

Printed primary sources

Accounts of the Lord High Treasurer of Scotland, **ii**, *1500–1504*, **iii**, *1506–1507*, ed J Balfour Paul (Edinburgh, 1900, 1901)

The Acts of the Lords Auditors of Causes and Complaints 1466–1494, ed T Thomson (London, 1839)

Acts of the Lords of Council in Public Affairs 1501–1554: Selections from Acta Dominorum Concilii, ed R K Hannay (Edinburgh, 1932)

Androw of Wyntoun's Orygynal Cronykil of Scotland, ed A Laing (Edinburgh, 1872–79)

'Bagimond's Roll – Statement of the Tenths of the Kingdom of Scotland', ed

A I Dunlop, *Miscellany of the Scottish History Society*, **vi** (SHS, 1939), 3–77

Calendar of Documents Relating to Scotland, ed J Bain, 4 vols (Edinburgh, 1881–88)

Calendar of Documents Relating to Scotland, **v**, *1108–1516* (Supplementary), eds G G Simpson and J D Galbraith (Edinburgh, 1985)

Daniell, W, *Daniell's Scotland: a Voyage around the Coast of Scotland and the Adjacent Isles, 1815–22*, 2 vols (Edinburgh, 2006)

Documents Illustrative of the History of Scotland 1286–1306, ed J Stevenson (Edinburgh, 1870)

The Dublin guild merchant roll, c.1190–1265, eds P Connolly and G Martin (Dublin, 1992)

The Exchequer Rolls of Scotland, ed J Stuart *et al* (Edinburgh, 1878–1908)

History of the Union of Scotland and England by Sir John Clerk of Pennicuik, trans and ed D Duncan (SHS, 1993)

The Knights of St John of Jerusalem in Scotland, eds I B Cowan, P H R Mackay and A Macquarrie (SHS, 1983)

Liber Quotidianus Contrarotulatoris Garderobae Anno Regni Edwardi Primi Vicesimo Octavo, ed J Topham (London, 1787)

Lindsay, A, *A Rutter of the Scottish Seas c.1540* (National Maritime Museum Mongraphs **44**, 1980)

Macfarlane, W, *Geographical Collections relating to Scotland*, eds A Mitchell and J T Clark, 2 vols (Edinburgh, 1906–08)

Pococke, *Tour through Scotland, 1760,* ed D W Kemp (SHS, Edinburgh, 1887)

Poor Law Inquiry Commission for Scotland (1844), Examinations, Synod of Galloway, Parish of Whithorn, 529

Regesta Regum Scotorum, **vi**, *The Acts of David II*, ed B Webster (Edinburgh, 1976)

Register of the Privy Council of Scotland, J H Burton *et al* (eds) (Edinburgh, 1877–1970)

'Register Containing the State and Condition of every Burgh within the Kingdom of Scotland … 1692', in *Miscellany of the Scottish Burgh Records Society* (Edinburgh, 1881)

Registrum Magni Sigilli Regum Scotorum, **i**, *1306–1424*, ed J M Thomson (repr Edinburgh, 1984)

Registrum Magni Sigilli Regum Scotorum, **ii**, *1424–1513*, ed J Balfour Paul (repr Edinburgh, 1984)

Registrum Magni Sigilli Regum Scotorum, **vii**

Registrum Magni Sigilli Regum Scotorum, **xi**

Registrum Secreti Sigilli Regum Scotorum, eds M Livingstone *et al* (Edinburgh, 1882–1914)

Report from Select Committee on Orange Institutions in Great Britain and the Colonies (1835)

Report upon the boundaries of the several cities burghs and towns of Scotland … 1832

'Report by Thomas Tucker upon the Settlement of the Revenues of Excise and Customs in Scotland. AD MDCLVI', in *Miscellany of the Scottish Burgh Records Society* (Edinburgh, 1881), 1–48

Rishanger, William, *Chronica et Annales*, ed H T Riley (London: Rolls Series, 1865)

Rotuli Scotiae in Turri Londiniensi et in Domo Capitulari Westmonasteriensi Asservati, eds D Macpherson *et al*, 2 vols (London, 1814–19)

The Statistical Account of Scotland 1791–1799, vol. 1, General, eds D J Withrington and I R Grant (Wakefield, 1983)

The Statistical Account of Scotland 1791–1799, vol. 5, Stewartry of Kirkcudbright and Wigtownshire, eds D J Withrington and I R Grant (Wakefield, 1983), 'Parish of Wigton', Revd Andrew Duncan, 1793

The Statistical Account of Scotland (Edinburgh, 1845), 'Parish of Wigton', Revd Peter Young, 1839

Smith, S, *General View of the Agriculture of Galloway* (London, 1810)

Symson, A, *A Large Description of Galloway by Andrew Symson, Minister of Kirkinner, 1684* (Edinburgh, 1823)

Third Statistical Account of Scotland, The County of Wigtown, ed M C Arnott (Glasgow, 1965), parish of Wigtown, Revd Gavin Lawson, 1949 and 1963)

A Tour through the whole Island of Great Britain, eds G D H Cole and D C Browning (London, 1962)

Webster, J, *General View of the Agriculture of Galloway* (Edinburgh, 1794)

Wigtown parish records. The session book of Wigtown, 1701–1745, ed H Paton (Edinburgh, 1934)

Wigtownshire Charters, ed R C Reid (SHS, 1960)

Works of reference

Catalogue of the National Museum of Antiquities of Scotland (new edn, Edinburgh, 1892)

Cowan, I B, *The Parishes of Medieval Scotland* (Scottish Record Society, 1967)

Cowan, I B, and Easson, D E, *Medieval Religious Houses: Scotland,* 2nd edition (London, 1976)

Groome, F, *Ordnance Gazetteer* (Glasgow, 1894–95)

Oxford Dictionary of National Biography, http://www.oxforddnb.com/

Pigot and Co's New Commercial Directory of Scotland for 1825–26, 1837 (London and Manchester)

Slater's Royal National Commercial Directory of Scotland … (Manchester and London, 1852, 1867, 1873, 1878, 1886, 1889, 1893, 1900, 1903, 1907, 1911, 1915)

The Topographical, Statistical and Historical Gazetteer of Scotland, 2 vols (Glasgow, 1842)

Secondary sources

Barnard, A, *The Whisky Distilleries of the United Kingdom* (1887, repr Newton Abbott, 1969)

Brann, J, '26 South Main Street, Wigtown (Wigtown parish), medieval burgh watching brief', *DES 1997*, 27

Brann, J, 'Wigtown, Dumfries and Galloway (Wigtown parish), watching briefs', *DES 2000*, 23

Brann, J, 'Harbour Road, Wigtown, Dumfries and Galloway (Wigtown parish), wall', *DES 2001*, 28

Brann, J, '11 North Main Street, Wigtown, Dumfries and Galloway (Wigtown parish), laird's town house', *DES 2001*, 29

Brewster, D, *Wigtown: the Story of a Royal and Ancient Burgh* (Newton Stewart, nd)

Brooke, D, 'Wigtown: profile of a medieval burgh', *TDGNHAS,* 3rd ser **60** (1985), 51–61

Brown, M, *The Black Douglases: war and lordship in late Medieval Scotland, 1300–1455* (East Linton, 1998)

Burgh of Wigtown, Official Guide (Croydon [1959])

Campbell, R H, *Owners and Occupiers: Changes in Rural Society in South-West Scotland before 1914* (Aberdeen, 1991)

Checkland, S G, *Scottish Banking: a history 1695–1973* (Glasgow & London, 1975)

Clough, T H McK and Cummins W A, 'Lists of identifications', in T H McK Clough, and W A Cummins, *Stone axe studies, volume 2: the petrology of prehistoric stone implements from the British Isles*, CBA Res Rep **67** (London, 1988)

Collingwood, W G, 'The Early Crosses of Galloway', *TDGNHAS,* 3rd ser **10** (1922–23), 221–3

Cormack, W F, 'Wigtown, Roman coin', *DES* 1967, 55

Cormack, W F, 'Wigtown burgh and parish 10 North Bank Street, inscribed and carved stones', *DES* 1983, 4

Dennison, E P, Gallagher, D, and Ewart, G, *Historic Maybole: Archaeology and Development* (CBA, York, 2005)

Devine, T M, *The Scottish Nation 1700–2000* (London, 1999)

Dick, C H, *Highways and Byways in Galloway and Carrick* (Edinburgh, 1924)

Donnachie, I, 'The Economy of Galloway in Historical Perspective', in *The Galloway Project: a Study of the Economy of South West Scotland with Particular Reference to its Tourist Potential* (Scottish Tourist Board, Edinburgh, 1968)

Donnachie, I, *The Industrial Archaeology of Galloway* (Newton Abbot, 1971)

Donnachie, I and MacLeod, I, *Old Galloway* (Newton Abbot, 1974)

Dow, F, *Cromwellian Scotland 1651–1660* (Edinburgh, 1979)

Duncan, A A M, *Scotland: the Making of the Kingdom* (Edinburgh, 1975)

Fraser, G, *Wigtown and Whithorn: Historical and Descriptive Sketches, Stories and Anecdotes, Illustrative of the Racy Wit and Pawky Humour of the District* (Wigtown, 1877)

Fraser, G, *Lowland Lore; or the Wigtownshire of long ago* (Wigtown, 1880)

Friel, I, *The Good Ship: Ships, Shipbuilding and technology in England 1200–1520* (London, 1995)

Gifford, J, *The Buildings of Scotland: Dumfries and Galloway* (London, 1996)

Graham, A, 'Some old harbours in Wigtownshire', *TDGNHAS,* 3rd ser **54** (1979)

Graham, E, *A Maritime History of Scotland* (East Linton, 2002)

Haggarty, A and Haggarty, G, 'Excavations at Rispain Camp, Whithorn, 1978–81', *TDGNHAS,* 3rd ser **58** (1985), 21–51

Hall, D, 'High Vennel, Wigtown (Wigtown parish)', *DES* 1992, 27

Handley, J E, *The Irish in Scotland 1798–1845* (Cork, 1945)

MacQueen, J, 'The Gaelic speakers of Galloway and Carrick', *Scottish Studies* **xvii** (1973), 17–33

M'Kerlie, P H, *History of the Lands and their Owners in Galloway*, 2 vols (Edinburgh, 1870, repr, ed Gardner, Paisley, 1906)

MacLeod, I, *Discovering Galloway* (Edinburgh, 1986)

McNeill, P G B and MacQueen, H L eds, *Atlas of Scottish History to 1707* (Edinburgh, 1996)

Malcolm, C, *The History of the British Linen Bank* (Edinburgh, 1950)

Martin, P, *Cupar: The History of a Small Scottish Town* (Edinburgh, 2006)

Maxwell, H E, 'Ancient weapons, instruments, utensils and ornaments of Wigtonshire. With list of the principal stone implements recorded from Wigtonshire', *Archaeol Hist Collect Ayrshire Galloway* **5** (1885), 51

Morrison, I, 'Galloway: Locality and Landscape Evolution', in R D Oram and G P Stell eds, *Galloway: Land and Lordship* (Edinburgh, 1991)

Muir, T S, *Ecclesiological Notes on some of the Islands of Scotland* (Edinburgh, 1885), 245

Munn, C, *The Scottish Provincial Banking Companies 1747–1864* (Edinburgh, 1981)

Murray, A, 'The Customs Accounts of Kirkcudbright, Wigtown and Dumfries, 1434–1560', *TDGNHAS*, 3rd ser **40** (1963), 136–62

Nix, V, '17 Agnew Crescent, Wigtown, Dumfries and Galloway (Wigtown parish), sculptured panel', *DES* 2001, 28

Noel, M, 'Black's Field, Wigtown (Wigtown parish), geophysical survey', *DES* 2003, 52

Oram, R D, 'Dervorgilla, the Balliols and Buittle', *TDGNHAS*, 3rd ser **73** (1999), 165–81

Oram, R D, *The Lordship of Galloway* (Edinburgh, 2000)

Oram, R D, '"It cannot be decernit quha is clene and quha is foulle". Responses to epidemic disease in 16th- and 17th-century Scotland', *Renaissance and Reformation* (2006)

Oram, R D, 'Abondance inépuisable? Crise de l'approvisionnement en combustible et réactions en Ecosse du Nord entre environ 1500 et environ 1800', in J-M Derex and F Gregoire, *Histoire économique et sociale de la tourbe et des tourbières*, Æstuaria: Cordemais (2009), 31–44

Oram, R D, Martin, P F, McKean, C A, Cathcart, A and Neighbour, T, *Historic Tain: Archaeology and Development* (CBA, York, 2009)

Oram, R D, Martin, P F, McKean, C A, and Anderson, S, *Historic Whithorn: Archaeology and Development* (CBA, York, 2010)

Penman, M A, *David II, 1329–71* (East Linton, 2004)

Ralegh Radford, C A, and Donaldson, G, *Whithorn and Kirkmadrine* (HMSO, 1953)

Reid, R C, 'Some notes on pre-Reformation Wigtown', *TDGNHAS*, 3rd ser **12** (1924–25), 241–2

Roe, F E S, 'The battle-axes, mace-heads and axe-hammers from south-west Scotland', *TDGNHAS*, 3rd ser **44** (1967), 80

Rorke, Gallagher, D, McKean, C, Dennison E P, and Ewart, G, *Historic Galashiels: Archaeology and Development* (CBA, York, 2011)

Royal Commission on the Ancient and Historical Monuments of Scotland, *Galloway vol i. Wigtownshire* (Edinburgh, 1912)

Royal Commission on the Ancient and Historical Monuments of Scotland, *Tolbooths and Townhouses: Civic Architecture in Scotland to 1833* (HMSO, 1996)

Simpson, A T and Stevenson, S, *Historic Wigtown: the archaeological implications of development* (Scottish burgh survey series, Glasgow, 1981)

Smith, D L, *The Little Railways of South-West Scotland* (Newton Abbot, 1969)

Smout, T C, *Scottish Trade on the Eve of Union, 1660–1707* (Edinburgh, 1963)

Smout, T C, *A History of the Scottish People* (London, 1985)

Stell, G, *Dumfries and Galloway* (HMSO, 1986)

Tayler, A and Tayler, H, *John Graham of Claverhouse* (London, 1939)

Taylor, W, *The Military Roads in Scotland* (Newton Abbot, 1976)

Towsey, M, '"All partners may be enlightened and improved by reading them": the distribution of Enlightenment books in Scottish subscription library catalogues, 1750–c.1820', *Journal of Scottish Historical Studies* **28**.1 (2008), 20–43

Truckell, A E, 'Wigtown Burgh Court Book, 1512–1535', *TDGNHAS*, 3rd ser **67** (1987), 66–9

Truckell, A E and Williams, J, 'Mediaeval pottery in Dumfriesshire and Galloway', *TDGNHAS*, 3rd ser **44** (1966–67), 133

Walker, G, 'The Protestant Irish in Scotland', in T M Devine ed, *Irish Immigrants and Scottish Society in the Nineteenth and Twentieth Centuries* (Edinburgh, 1991), 44–66

Wigtown: a Parish History (1988)

Wigtown's Historic Buildings, Wigtown and Bladnoch Business Association (Wigtown, nd)

Wigtownshire Official Guide (Dundee [1955])

Wilson, G, 'Notice of a collection of implements of stone and bronze, now presented to the museum, and exhibited to the meeting, and other Antiquities from Wigtownshire', *PSAS* **14** (1879–80), 126–7

Wilson, J, *Voyage round the Coasts of Scotland* (Edinburgh, 1842)

Unpublished sources

Birchman, J E, typescript record of Wigtown Old Churchyard, Tombstone Inscriptions (1981)

Hill, C, The Maritime Economy of Dumfries and Galloway, 1707–1850 (PhD thesis, University of Strathclyde, 2004)

Ramsay, S, Miller, J, and Housely, R, Whithorn Environs: Palaeoenvironmental Investigation of Rispain Mire (First draft, Dept of Archaeology, University of Glasgow, nd)

Townscape Heritage Research Unit, Dept of Planning, Townscape Heritage Initiative Schemes Evaluation, Wigtown (Oxford Brookes University, 2007)

Index

Numbers in **bold** refer to figures, maps or their captions